Power Carving BOOTS & SHOES

Roman Hrytsak

Schiffer Publishing Ltd
4880 Lower Valley Road • Atglen, PA 19310

Dedication

I dedicate this book to those who are most important in my life, my immediate family. First, to my wife, Marjorie: much gratitude for her constant support and encouragement. This had a major impact in expanding my bounds of creativity. Second, to my first-generation, eldest son John, and his wife Kristen, and my second son Michael, and his wife Kim: for allowing me to see life and beauty through their eyes. Third, to my second-generation, Olivia, Quinn, Brynn, and Faryn: four little ones that keep me thinking and being young!

Library of Congress Control Number: 2014938136

Title Page Photo Caption: introduction to a "Roman style" boot. In the left image, Pine beetle damage can be seen in the design of the boot.

Designed by Matt Goodman
Type set in Helvetica

ISBN: 978-0-7643-4615-6
Printed in China

Published by Schiffer Publishing, Ltd.
4880 Lower Valley Road
Atglen, PA 19310
Phone: (610) 593-1777; Fax: (610) 593-2002
E-mail: Info@schifferbooks.com

Contents

Introduction

Why Wooden Boots & Shoes?

Wren and boot – tupelo; Base – walnut

My carving career started in 1990 when my wife encouraged me to take a power-carving class, hoping to de-stress me from my high-powered sales job. It was a class for carving song-birds, and more proficient carvers than I chose to carve a Western Meadowlark. In my naivete, and with my one-hundred-dollar power carver and a short assembly of burrs and bits, I jumped into the sawdust, completing the project after twelve hours of instruction. Entitled *Prairie Song*, the piece is a favorite of the family and is proudly displayed in our home.

A growing confidence and proficiency in carving led to excitement along the learning curve and I was forever hooked to this form of art expression. After many instruction classes, the projects increased, as did the accumulation of power-carving tools. Mastering detailed instructions and patterns in bird-carving, I soon moved to other carving projects. Here I found more interest in stylized, free-form carving. Leaving the strictness of technical details behind, a new expression in creativity occurred.

A commission for a house wren provided me the opportunity I wanted. I was not satisfied with some of the suggested mounts shown in carving books, so I decided on another approach. Why not a worn, wrinkled, dried-out, ankle-high leather boot? The image of the boot came from the style of shoe I wore as a youngster growing up on the family farm. The ankle-style boots, with sewn leather tops and soles, would have undergone considerable wear throughout the year. This added much character to the boot.

Stylized pine

Willow

Spalted Mayday

Pine, Willow, Maple

The stretch and strain of a year's wear and tear made the boots non-reparable. My faithful friends were soon relinquished for another use. Tied up discreetly to a tree branch, the boot became a birdhouse and most of the time it was the house wren that made the first claim.

One of my greatest joys was seeing a family of wrens occupying a wrinkled old boot with a worn-out sole and no laces. This is the image I had when I created my first wooden boot.

After completing the wren carving, the daunting task of making the mount was upon me. I wanted some character in this boot, so I glued together some left-over pieces of tupelo wood. With a rough sketch for a pattern and a lot of imagination, the boot came into being. Detailing and texturing techniques I had learned from my bird-carving were adopted to the boot. Since I was going to paint the boot, I was not concerned about glue lines.

It was easy carving the exterior of the boot blank, but the interior part became the challenge. Having carved and glued pieces of wood in my first wren boot, a technique evolved where I would cut the blank into three parts relevant to the boot. These parts would then be rough carved for shape and style, refined and detailed, finished, and re-assembled.

I was fortunate to have access to many types of wood, mostly cutoffs and discards due to checks, splits, and knots. What was considered "garbage wood" to professional woodworkers was a treasure trove to me. Soon, my wood bin was flooded with a variety of wood species. What followed was continued experimentation with figure and grain, coupled with shapes and forms.

An interesting and unique caricature of a work boot was the result. As time went by, the 'wren boot' evolved so that the boot creation could now stand alone as a work of art.

Chapter 1:

Getting Ready to Carve

Amur cherry log with boot

Wood Selection

Selecting wood for your boot is entirely your choice. To make the boot a one-of-a-kind creation, select wood with interesting patterns and figures. Tracing your boot pattern either with the grain or across the grain will depend on the block size. Choosing a hard wood or a soft wood will make a good boot.

Whatever the choice, ensure that the wood is squared off to allow for a safe cut when making your boot blank. With many checks or splits in your wood, you may wish to reinforce the starting block with white or two-part epoxy glue. Choice of glue will depend on how quickly you want to get on with the project. If the splits are too great, this choice of wood should be abandoned, as the fragility will create problems during the cutting and carving process.

Laminations can also be used to create different grain patterns with a variety of exotic and interesting wood. The limitation here is one's imagination. Plainer type wood, where the grain is not too prominent, can be textured and detailed with your ruby carving bits or a pyrography tool. Contrasting dyes and stains are other options to incorporate into your boot.

Arbutus wood

Tools and Shop Safety

The tools that I use in my carving work are predominantly power tools.

First is the **bandsaw**. It's major use is to re-saw rough wood for preparing the blank. A narrow blade width measuring from 1/4" to 3/8" is beneficial to cut out the blank and to make tight sharp turns in small areas.

The **power-carving tools** are small motors capable of generating 3500 to 18,000 RPM, and are powerful enough to remove wood rapidly using carving burrs. These burrs are fastened by a collet to a handpiece, which, in turn, are connected to the power source via a flex-shaft. The handpiece has interchangeable collets in order to handle the various shaft sizes of each bit. Which bit is used depends on the stage of the carving process.

Carving **knives**, **chisels** and **gouges**, and **small rasps** can also be used to remove wood. Refining leaves the boot blank in a fragile state, but a set of small wood clamps and vises to serve as shoe lasts allows the hand-carving to proceed without too many mishaps.

A set of **calipers** for measuring thickness and depth is useful, but not essential. A **measuring tape** helps if you are to replicate a piece. Finally, a **pencil** and **sketch pad** can prove to be the most useful tool in your workshop. Capturing your one-of-a-kind design on paper will help you to create a pattern, showing guidelines for the carving process. See page 55 for examples of boot styles and sketches.

Since there will be glue-ups, a **vise** and some **clamps** are beneficial.

One major drawback of power tools is that there is a lot of sawdust and fine dust created in the carving process. **Face masks**, **adequate ventilation**, and **vacuum systems** are essential to ensure good health now and in the future. **Safety glasses** are also a must, for protecting your eyes from injury.

There are hazards with all of the tools listed. One should remove any distractions, so that the carving process will be most enjoyable.

Chapter 2:

Block to Blank to Boot

Split rail cedar fence post morphs into a boot.

Making the Pattern

Side profile

Top profile

Front profile

Rear profile

Side/bottom profile

Using your boot model and a sketch pad, make a rough drawing of the boot showing a side, top, front, and rear profile. This will be the start to your pattern development.

In making your pattern, describe the boot sections using the following terms: the **SOLE**, which includes both the sole and heel; the **TOE**, which includes the toe cap and tongue; and the **VAMP**, which includes the ankle and leg cover, along with the lace-up area.

BLOCK TO BLANK PROFILES
Points to Consider in Making a Pattern

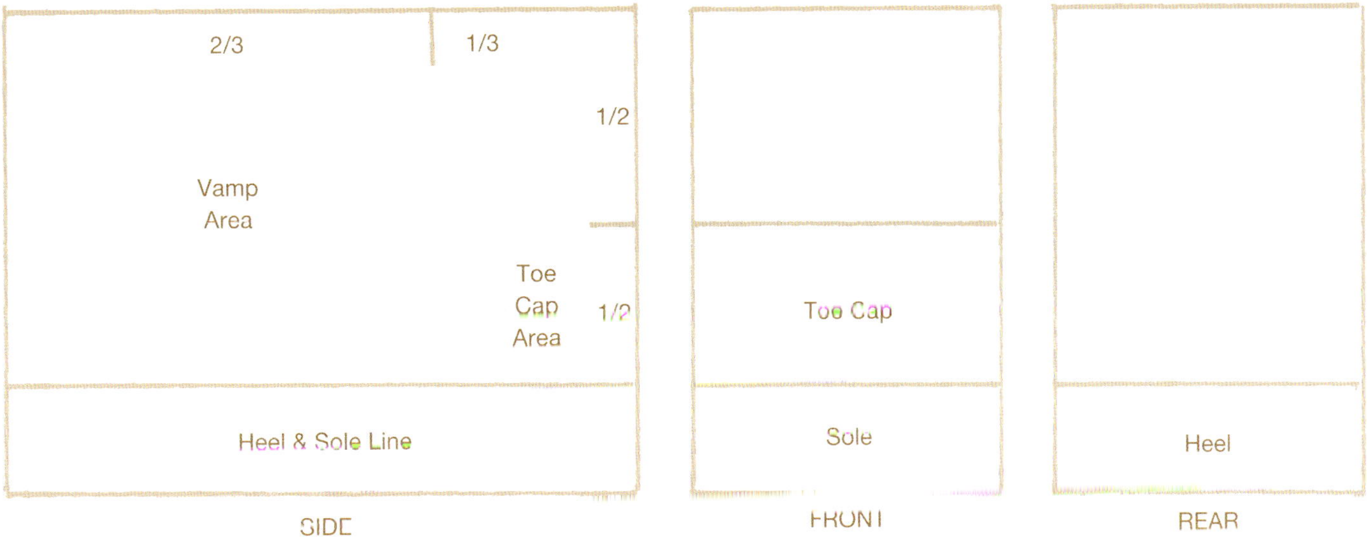

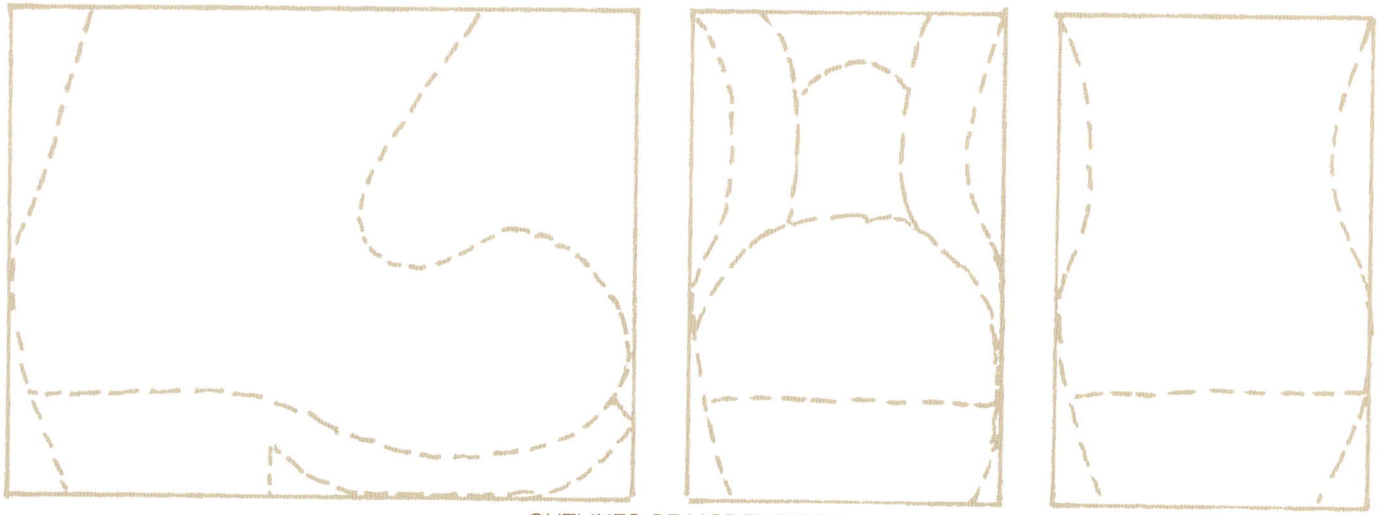

OUTLINES OF MODEL BOOT

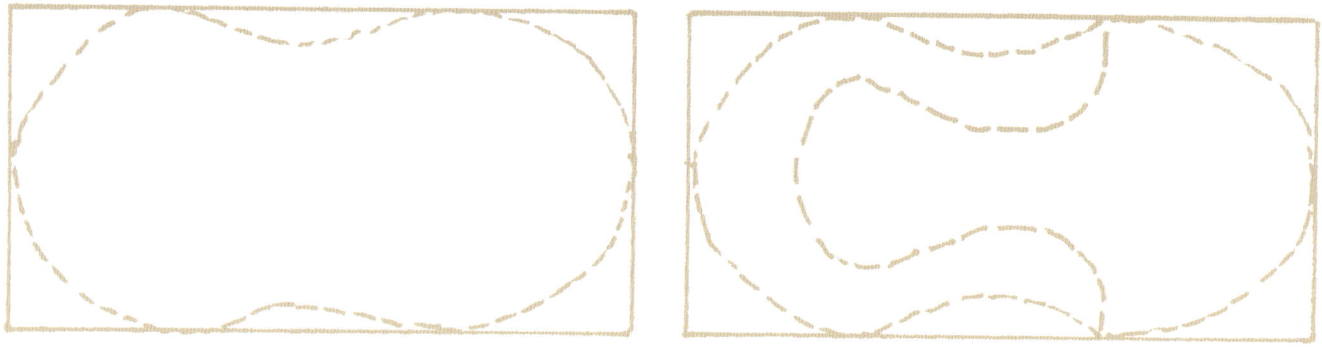

BLANK IN THREE PARTS

For your pattern, the length-wise proportion of the boot section, i.e. **VAMP**, should be kept to two-thirds of the full length. When tracing this measurement on your block of wood, this proportion may seem large, but it's necessary if you are going to give the lace-up area some stretch to extend the upper vamp area.

The **TOE** section in your pattern can take the remaining third of the boot length and, in some cases, depending on your piece of wood, the toe can be extended length-wise and/or be curved upward to show a bend in your boot.

Milled wood squared off for the bandsaw cuts

Spalted birch

Maple

Maple

Beginning your "Roman style" boot, a block of wood with the approximate measurements of 7" in length, 4" in width, and 5" in height is a good start. During the carving process, you will lose 15 to 20 percent of the wood. Preferably the block should be squared off to enable you to make safe cuts with your bandsaw.

Details such as lace eyelets, wrinkles, stitching, wear and tear marks, etc. are optional and can be added at the refining stage. The wood chosen will dictate whether or not detailing and texturing will add to the composition. Keep your design and details simple. Let the wood "speak" to you!

Blank Preparation

You can chose to trace your pattern from your drawing or do it free-hand on the block of wood. Using your bandsaw, cut along the side and top profile lines. This will remove wood from the front and rear of the boot, giving you the first view of a rough cut boot blank.

At this time, small trim cuts can be made to remove wood to define the heel/sole notch and the front sole curvature. It is easier to do these trim cuts when the sole is still connected to the boot blank.

BANDSAW CUT LINES WHEN DESIGNING BOOT PATTERN

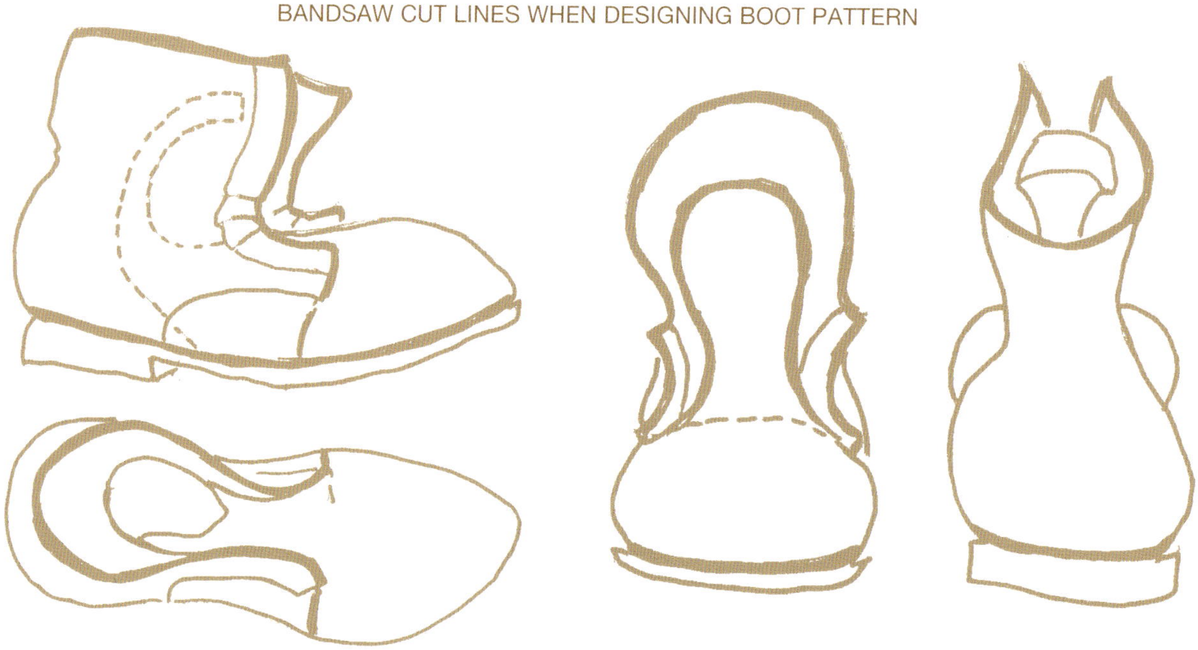

Pattern on block showing side, top, and front profiles.

Bandsaw cuts expose rough shape of boot.

Side wood is removed, showing the boot's curvature.

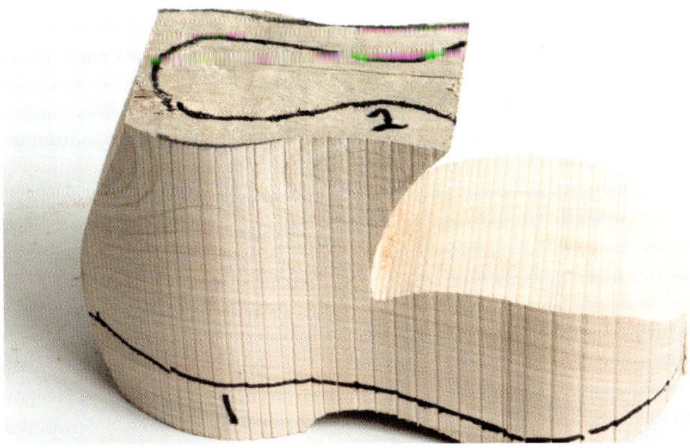

Sole cut line and upper vamp cut line ("omega shaped")

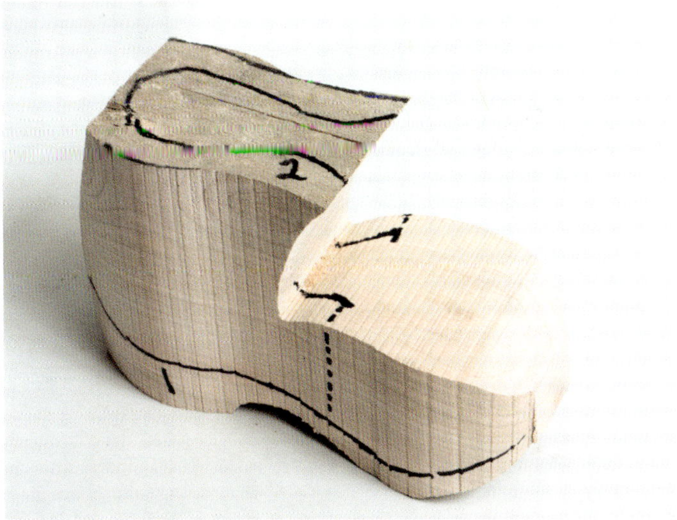

The upper cut line is defined.

Bandsaw cut is made.

Continuing the refinement of the boot blank, place the blank on its side and cut along the sole section line to separate the blank into two pieces. This is a major cut in preparing your blank and is the introduction to the procedure followed in carving a "Roman style" boot. The importance of this cut will become evident and show its relevance during the carving stages.

The sole, if not pre-trimmed for shape and size, will have a somewhat rectangular shape with the heel area being the thicker part. Place the sole/heel piece aside and have it ready for carving after the upper boot parts are roughed out and refined.

Now, back to the boot blank proper: With the boot blank in an upright position, an "omega shaped" line will show the top profile for the vamp section of the boot. The curvature of this line defines the walls of the upper part of the boot. These lines lead to the front of the boot, dropping along the front of the vamp or lace-up area and then move forward about 1/2" to 3/4" along the toe cap, and then move in a slow curve to the outer side edges of the toe cap. Herein is the line for your second major cut to make a "Roman style" boot.

Three parts to boot blank: Bandsaw cut no. 1 -- Sole separation; Bandsaw cut No. 2 -- Vamp separated from Tongue/ toe cap, providing two parts.

Using your bandsaw, making a cut along this line will separate the vamp section from the toe cap/tongue section. You can now see the relevance of removing the sole first. The sole section is the main foundation of the boot where the re-assembling of your boot pieces occurs. Cutting the vamp and toe sections first, destroys the foundation of your boot! The second point of relevance at this time is about the bandsaw blade. The upper profile requires some tight corner cuts so a narrow width blade is most useful. This cut opens up the inner part of the boot and defines the tongue.

Tongue wood refined – Bandsaw cut No. 3 and No. 4

Keep your vamp wall at about three eighths of an inch to one half an inch in thickness. Leave slightly more thickness at the back of the vamp. This will give you enough wood to carve inwards, in effect moving the back wall forward. Keep referring to your model and/or pattern for guidance. After carving, the upper vamp edge will be thinned out to about an eighth of an inch in thickness, while the bottom edge should not be less than one quarter of an inch in thickness. Staying close to these measurements will give you strength at the top and enough surface for a glue-up at the bottom.

With the toe section on it's side, carefully remove a small wedge of wood from the front of the tongue. This will push the tongue deeper into the boot. With the toe piece still on its side, carefully remove and round out the back of the tongue. This trim cut opens up the back interior part of the boot and also provides an area for some creativity to shape and bend the tongue.

Front view showing square tip of tongue wood.

The bandsaw or power-carver can be used for further removal of wood by rounding the corners of the back portions of the vamp and the front of the toe section.

Now you have a rough blank of the wooden boot. Put all the pieces together and mark the reference lines, where the pieces are to fit at the re-assembling stage. As the carving proceeds, you might need to re-draw these reference lines to ensure the proper fit. Wood blemishes and grain lines can all be useful as markers for the final match-up.

The **BLOCK** of wood has now had its first wood reduction and the **BLANK** is ready for roughing out.

Roughing Out the Blank

NO carving on sole and bottom vamp line.

NO carving at toe cap/vamp interface.

Before you start to carve away the excess wood to shape the blank into a boot, adopt and religiously follow the first rule in carving a "Roman style" boot: ***Do Not Carve on your kerf line at the sole and boot connection and at the kerf line separating the toe and vamp sections.*** This is where the glue is applied for re-assembly. Carving at these interfaces will affect the fit and look of the final boot.

REFINING THE BLANK

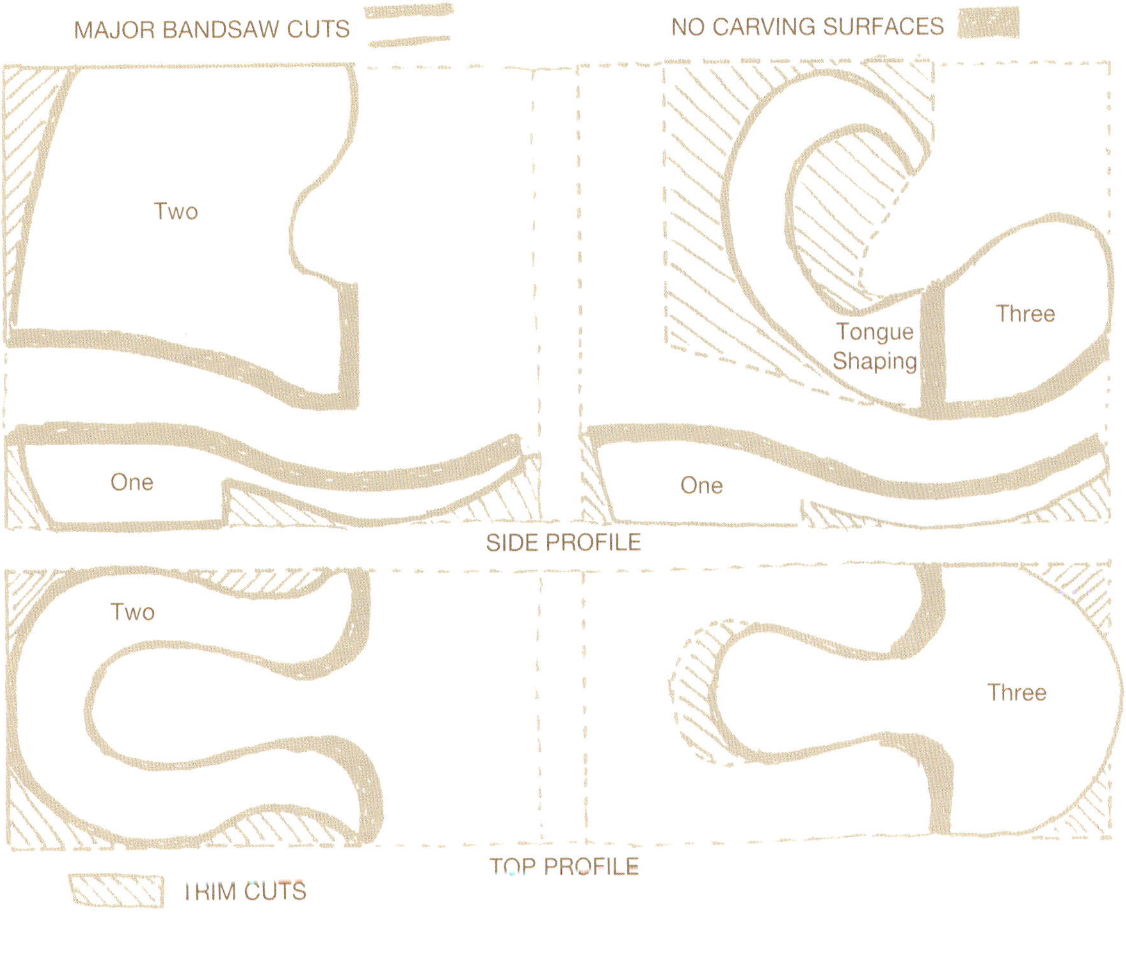

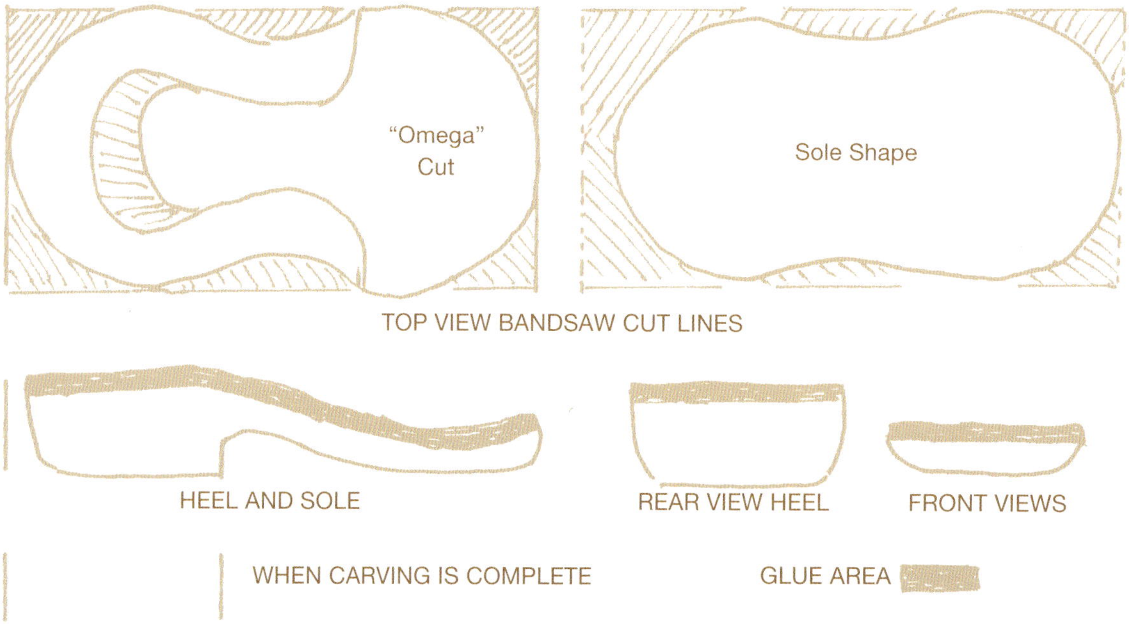

Separating the blank into three pieces allows the carver to use his burrs more efficiently and be more creative in affecting style and design. At the inner vamp area, you can maneuver your carving burrs easier, minimizing the possibility of a jam and a mishap.

Hash marks on the left blank shows area to be carved on the upper vamp compared to the completed boot on the right.

Hash marks at lace-up area

Rear hash marks

Now the fun begins! Start planning your carving strategy by drawing in potential finish lines. Wood type, grain, color, blemishes, etc., all play a role in your shaping and design.

Using your model as a guide, draw in hash marks to guide your wood removal. The composition of the boot is now in your hands. With your carving burrs, wood can be removed easily and rapidly and the vamp starts to take form.

Remove the outer wood at the top, which, in effect, pushes the shoe wall inward toward the tongue and defines the back and sides of the boot. At the front of the vamp, where it wraps around the tongue, you may want to carve the wall outward or leave it as tight and closed up to create mystery of what's beyond the tongue.

Where the vamp meets the toe section will depend on how you round out the toe. Remember these two areas should fit as tight as possible at the re-fit.

Rear and side view carving areas

Hash marks compared to finished boot

Round toe cap to fit rounding of vamp

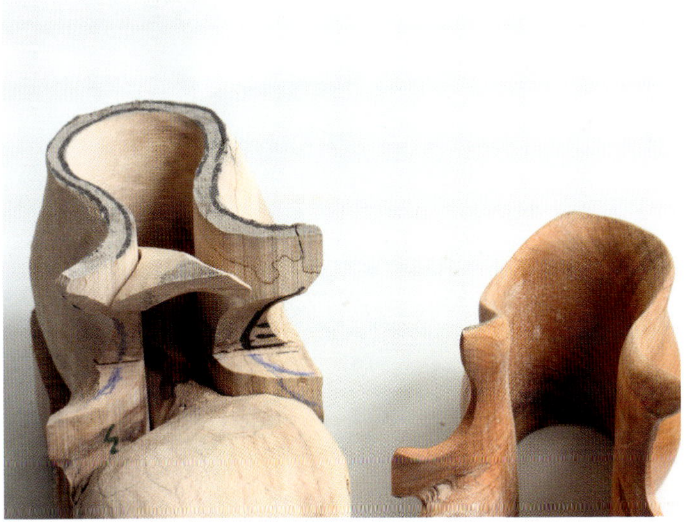

Blue lines for suggested reveal

The tongue can now be shaped. Usually after the bandsaw cut, the tongue will show four sides and also four corners.

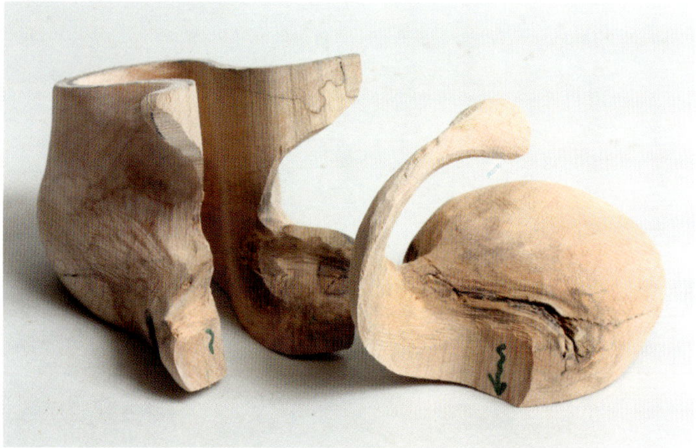

Tongue wood refined

Tongue/vamp refinement

This is where you can put some twist into the tongue when you are refining this area. Look at the boot from the front and decide which opposing corners you want to smooth out. Care must be taken here, though, as you are carving a thin strip of cross-grain. If a break is to occur, this is one area where it will happen. Many design changes have occurred at this stage. A two-part epoxy glue has staved off many mishaps. Go slow and easy.

Commence a small rounding of the edge where the vamp and toe sections meet the sole. This is not the final edge, but it will give you an idea for the shape of the sole. Care must be taken to leave an adequate bottom edge for a good glue-up to occur.

Vamp edge meeting sole is slightly rounded

Side view showing slight rounding of upper pieces at sole/vamp juncture

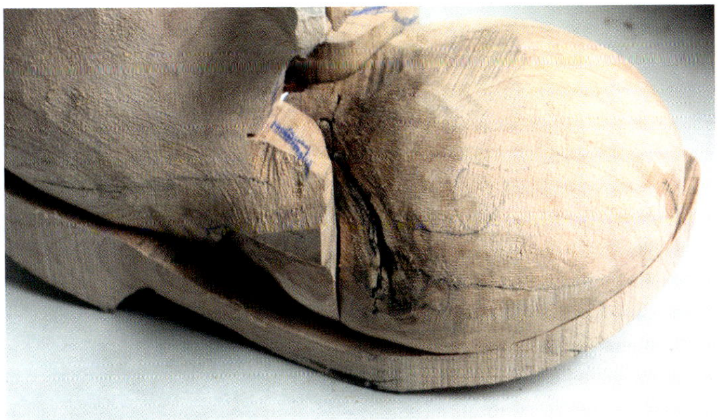
Sole refinement line

Refining toe cap vamp connection

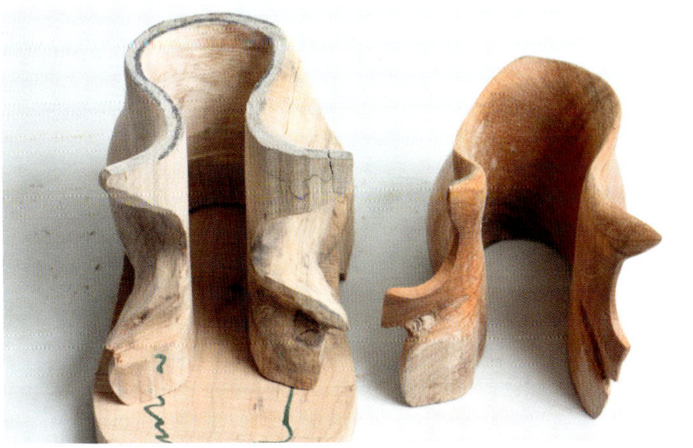
More refinement to make a good fit

Loosely assemble the upper parts of the boot and place them on the sole section ensuring that the reference marks match up. Trace the boot blank onto the sole piece.

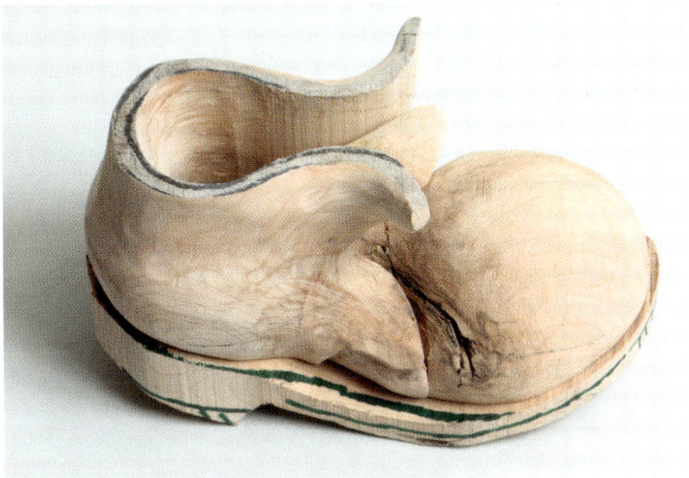
Defining the sole using refined upper pieces

Trim the sole piece. After removing the excess wood, re-mark and ensure that your reference lines meet accurately. Establish your heel size and refine to fit the rounding of the vamp.

Shaping the sole to meet the upper boot parts

Trim lines (Solid dark green lines)

Trimming the sole

Mark out the amount of roughing that is required to give a curvature to the bottom of the sole. A sharp edge gives a realistic worn look to the boot's sole and heel. At this time, a very light sanding to the saw kerf glue lines can be made to ensure a tight clean fit at the re-assembly stage.

Front view of sole bottom

Hash marks showing trim area on the sole and heel

Side view of sole trim area

Where the vamp meets the toe section, care must be taken to round out the two sections the same amount. If the rounding is a bit off, create a reveal that will distract the viewer from the joint.

Boot Refining

It is here that you will be making some decisions about details to give the boot its own character. What happens at this stage will depend on your creativity, your model, and your imagination. This is where you go for it! Your own detailing, wood selection, and physical characteristics will all play a role in what the final piece will look like.

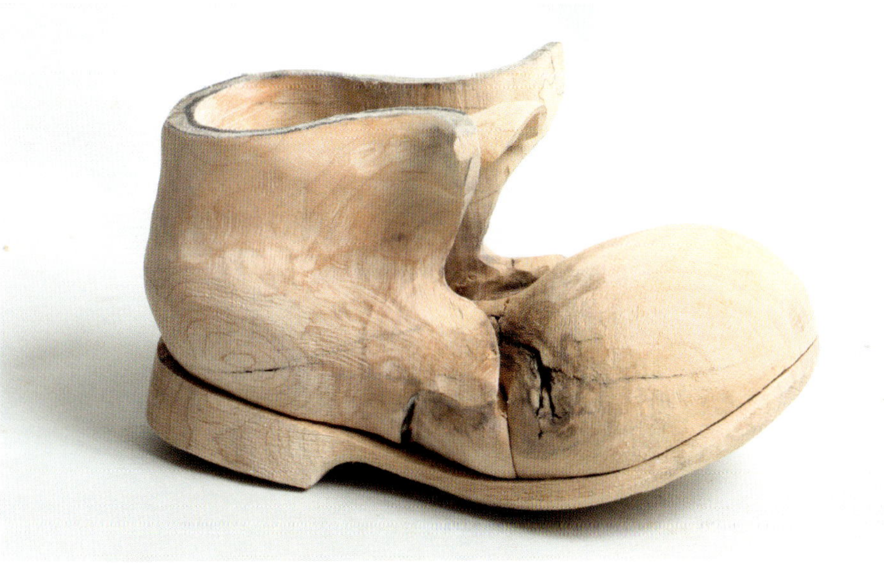

Carving complete, right profile

Carving complete, left profile

Carving complete, rear view

Sanded Boot

If the carving at this stage is to your liking, then the finishing stage is next. Power tools are great for removing wood, but they also leave a surface that requires some work before sealants and finishes can be applied. Clean up the fuzz, roughness, and scratches left by the burrs. Sanding with various grits of sandpaper is required or you will be disappointed with the finish. Establish direction of the grain and sand accordingly.

It makes the work easier if the sanding is done before you glue the pieces together. A drum sander attached to the power tool is most useful, but the final finish is accomplished with hand-sanding. This is tedious work, but it will be worth it in the end. With all pieces sanded, sealed, and varnished, the Blank has now entered the Boot stage. The assembly can now begin.

Boot Re-assembling

Before the pieces are glued together, you may wish to inscribe your name inside the boot. Regular carpenter's glue can be used, as well as a two-part epoxy glue. This type of glue sets up quickly, giving you a chance to do any final adjustments. Be conservative with the glue and avoid sloppy glue joints. Finally, give the boot a wax polish. This process protects the boot from frequent handling and helps to show off the grain.

You may wish to leave the inner part of the boot dull by using a ruby carver or stone for a rough texture. Hit it with a light sanding to remove any fuzz. Seal with a matte finish and the interior of the boot is complete. For contrast, a darker wood stain can be applied to enhance the appearance. This process is easier done when the pieces are still separate.

You can be assured that when the boot is on display, there will be many admirers who will want to handle the piece. These boots are very tactile.

Chapter 3:

The Next Step

Mastering the technique of shaping and stylizing a boot soon confronts one with new challenges. Exhausting the use of various shapes and species of wood, there are new paths to follow and new techniques to employ. The following text and pictures are some new ideas I would like to share with you.

Cedar boot, rough textured inner part of boot, with smooth surface outside

Reveal and Decorate

From my bird-carving, I used many techniques to "bump" and texture the wood surfaces for an effect. This is what I mean by a "reveal." Boot structure, lace eyelets, wrinkles, and sewing lines can be incorporated into your piece. Using your model, draw in some details and carve distinct surfaces to simulate these areas.

Cedar boot, lace-up eyelets and thread details

Cedar boot, various views

My first example is a pair of cedar wood boots I have titled *CHARLIE*. I was given several cutoffs from some cedar fence posts. These had a 4" x 4" dimension and a 16" length. Pondering the length, I soon came up with a boot that had an extended toe section. The grain was rather plain, so I decided to take a chance with some reveal work and texturing. The result was an almost matching pair of boots honoring one of my favorite celebrities — Charlie Chaplin. I recalled the unique shuffle he had in his walk, as well as the fact that he had a severe case of bunions. This was incorporated into the final design of the boots.

Brogues, textured and revealed

Brogues, another view

One of my favorite pair of boots was a pair of "Brogues," bought during my honeymoon to Yorkshire, England. To break them in, my father-in-law made me walk in them for a full day and step into as many puddles as I could. I was sure they would be ruined. However, the water and the walking shaped them to my foot perfectly. They were my constant footwear for over ten years until the cobbler could not re-sole them again. I have had other brogues, but none came to be enjoyed as much as those from Yorkshire. With a small piece of Amur cherry, my brogues were shaped to express their wrinkled and bent appearance.

Myrtle wood with gunstock orange stain and matte finish

Myrtle wood laminate

Sometimes I come into possession of beautiful wood, but the dimensions are short. With the two pieces of myrtle wood, I matched the grain and laminated the wood using carpenter's glue. Even with the lamination there was barely enough wood, but just enough to make a small boot showing wrinkles

Again, with a sizable length of Amur cherry, this boot was crafted using the two textures of bark and a smooth cut, exposing some beautiful grain and intermittent dark colors. The length of the piece of wood was enough for a woman's high-cut hiking boot. To give some balance to the contrasting textures, I decorated the boot with brass studs for buttons. A pyrography tool was used to make the button holes. This boot is called the *Cobra*.

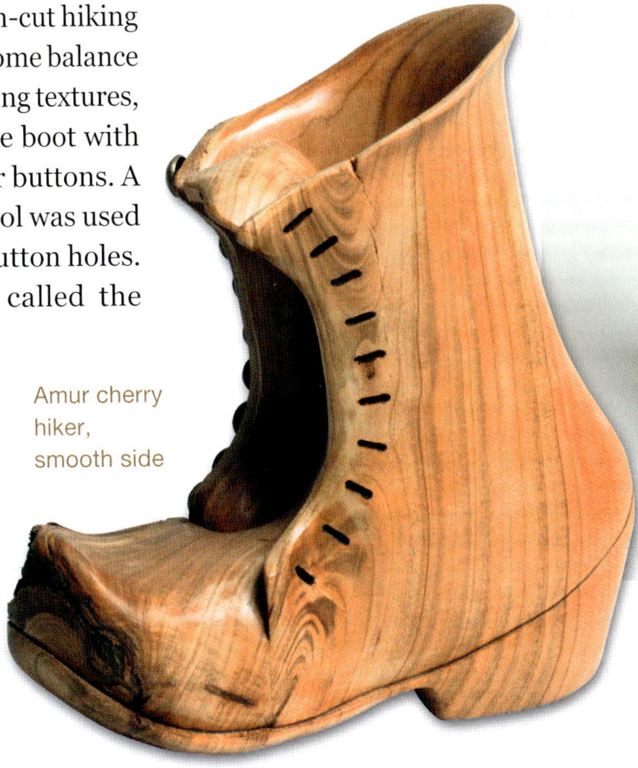

Amur cherry hiker, smooth side

Amur cherry hiker, *Cobra*

Soft slipper, "Mr. Casual"

Using a new technique for cutting the blank, a piece of mahogany taken from a discarded pallet came into my possession. Instead of making a boot with lace-ups a variation on a theme occurred. After the sole section was removed, a spade bit was used to remove the inner vamp wood. The size of the bit should allow for enough wood to be removed to carve the inner vamp area and leave enough wood for shaping the outer wall. Stained with gunstock orange and textured with a pyrography tool 'Mr. Casual' is the result.

Arbutus high heel

Slick Arbutus high heel

Using the same technique with a spade bit, a design was crafted to extend the heel. Arbutus wood with its twists and turns was my first women's boot - a caricature of a high heel with open toe and open heel.

Willow open toe and heel

This was followed with another high heel made from the trimmings of my willow tree. The toe section has the bark left on, showing where a branch had once been — a natural clear stain was used to highlight the bark's color.

Willow high heel

Maple high heel with bling

Some wood whimsy: a child's high heel with bling and a puzzle. Both are made from maple wood.

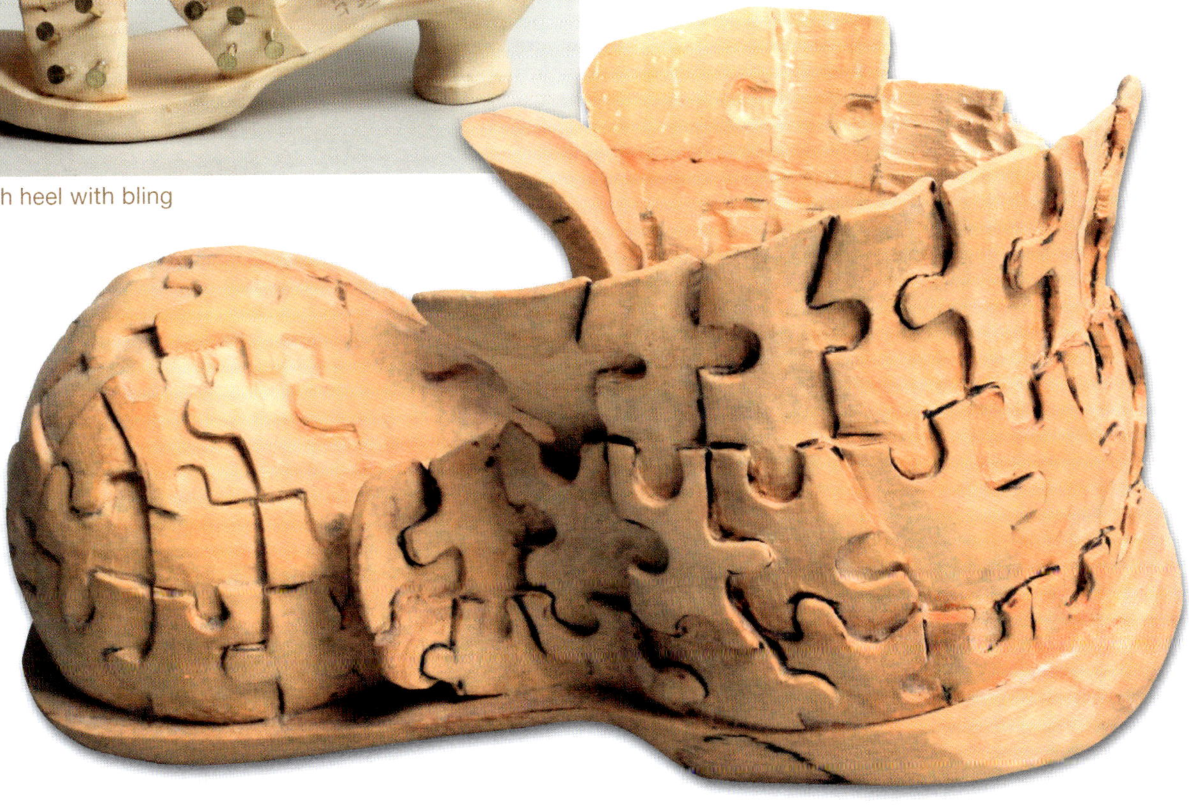

Maple puzzle

Chapter 4:

Carving a Stylized Wooden Boot

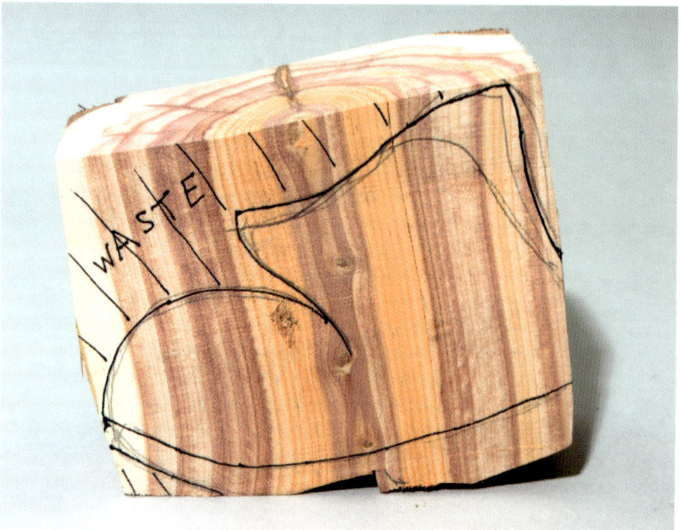

A stylized wooden boot with minimum detail is carved using a block of Rocky Mountain juniper wood. Block sized approximately 3" wide, 6" long, and 6" high. Using a leather boot as a model, draw a pattern side and top profiles, along with the sole/heel line.

STEP 1: Choose your wood and select a pattern. Boot side profile is drawn, along with the sole/heel line. Hash marks show waste wood to be removed.

STEP 2: With a bandsaw, cut away waste wood. The blank is defined.

STEP 3: With a bandsaw, make a horizontal cut along the sole line. This separates the sole/heel section from the upper boot block. This is the first – and most important – cut to be made for the boot blank. Next, make a vertical cut midway across the block; this separates the vamp from the toe/tongue section. The boot blank is now in three pieces and ready for rough carving.

STEP 4: Extra bandsaw cuts to refine the tongue. Removing wood from the front of the tongue helps to push the tongue into the shoe. Removing wood from the back of the tongue opens the interior space of the boot.

Frontal view of tongue – first shaping of tongue starts with bandsaw cut.

This tongue refinement leaves the tongue wood with four sides and four edges. Discussion as to how these surfaces should be carved and shaped will come later in the project.

STEP 5: Using a power tool equipped with a carving burr, round out the edges and square corners of the boot blank following the hash marks.

The upper vamp edge and lace-up edge should be no less than a 1/4" and the lower vamp edge should be at least 1/2" in thickness. This extra wood allows for further refinement and shaping later on in the project.

STEP 6: Following the hash marks, round the front of the toe section with your power-carver.

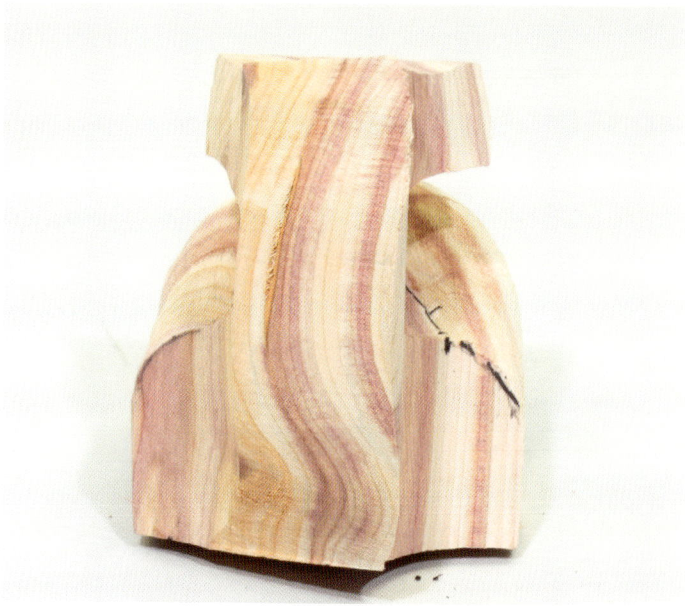

These images show the toe cap rounding extended to the back edge of the toe cap to fit rounding of the vamp notch.

Rounded toe cap guides the rounding of the vamp notch.

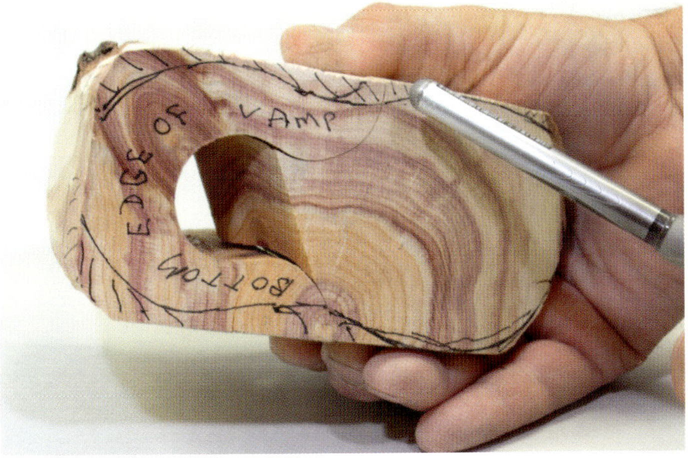

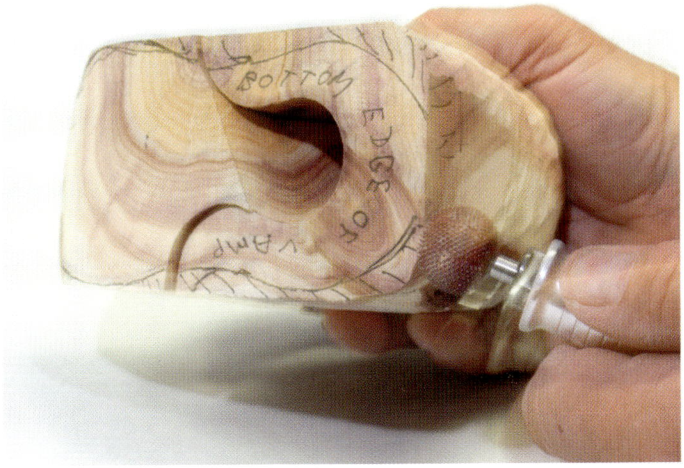

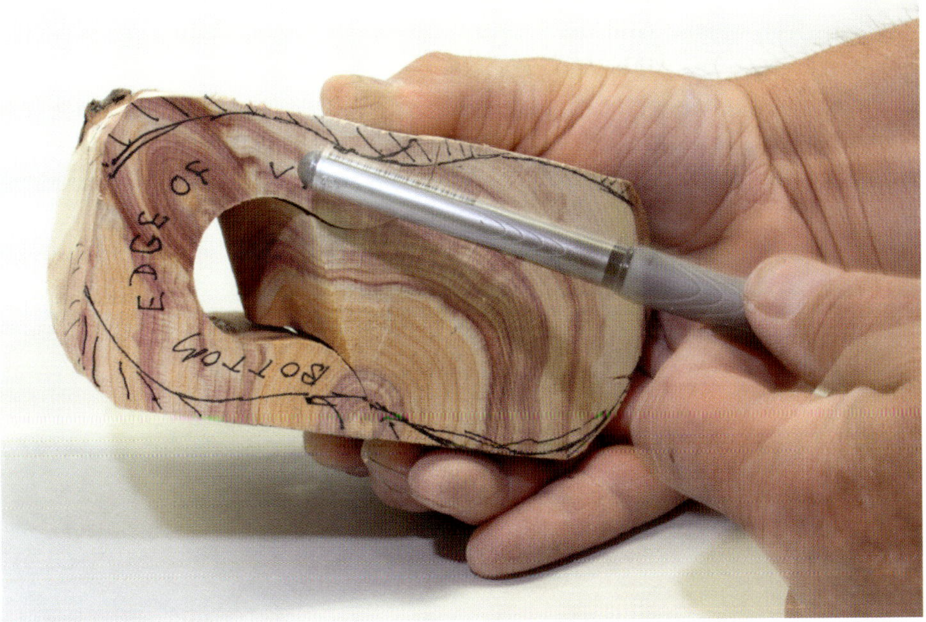

STEP 7: Bottom edge of boot drawn while the vamp and toe sections are held together. Following the hash marks, the bottom outer edge of the boot is defined with the power-carver. Bottom vamp edge width range 1/4" to 1/2".

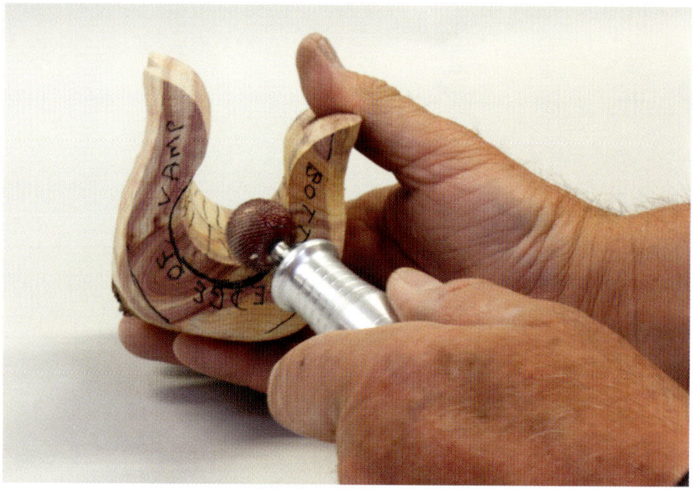

Lower inner vamp refined to expand inner space; power-carve along the hash marks.

STEP 8: Rounded upper boot sections placed on the sole/heel section. Boot shape traced onto sole piece, vertical edge of sole is carved.

Sole thickness established. Carve along hash marks to round out bottom of sole.

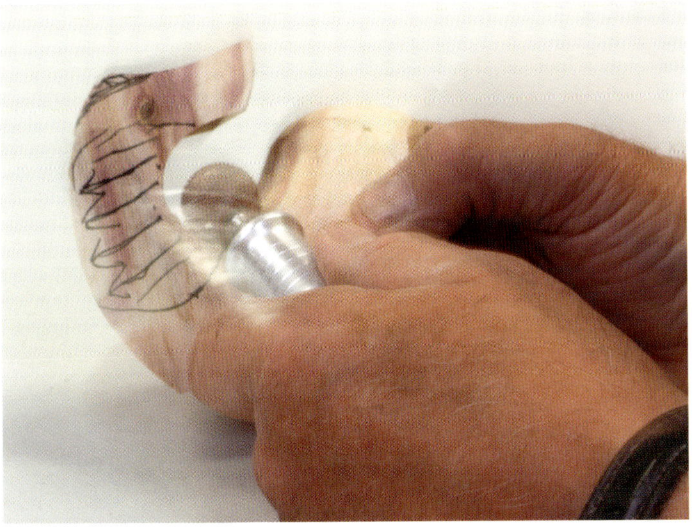

STEP 9: Tongue wood rough-carved to show two sides and two edges, reduced from four sides and four edges.

Tongue wood with final shaping.

The center wood is left thick enough for strength.

Draw a center line along the length of the tongue to use as a guide for refinement. The carving of the boot should now be complete.

STEP 10: A sanding drum removes the rough carving marks efficiently. Hand-sanding is used in difficult areas.

STEP 11: With sanding completed, the individual pieces are loosely assembled to check for fit. A sealant can be applied to the wood.

Further finishing with fine steel wool and fine grit sand paper completes the job. A finish coat can now be applied. It is easier to apply the finish to the individual pieces than finishing an assembled boot.

STEP 12: First stage of boot re-assembly. Two-part epoxy glue allows for a quick set. Boot vamp and toe section glued together first using the sole piece as a platform.

Check for fit and glue smears. Sand the kerf line for a good fit.

Final reassembly – glue the upper boot section to the sole/heel section using two-part epoxy.
Hold together or clamp gently to hold pieces until glue sets.

Apply wax finish and polish . . .
The project is complete.

Chapter 5

Carving a Detailed & Textured Lady's Brogue

A lady's brogue boot using basswood is the selected project. The starting block measured 4" wide, 7" long, and 2-1/2" high. Since this is not a lace-up style boot, a 2-1/2" depth is adequate and the "omega" cut was not required to separate the vamp from the toe section.

STEP 1: First bandsaw cut defines the boot shape and style. A brogue-style pattern was used to cut and shape a carving blank. An upper vamp line was drawn on the upper surface of the boot blank as well as a sole/heel line.

STEP 2: Second bandsaw cut is made along the sole/heel line to separate the block into a boot piece and a sole piece. Place the sole piece aside for carving later on in the project. Using a spade or Forstner bit, remove the vamp wood. Ensure that the vamp walls are at least 1/4" in thickness.

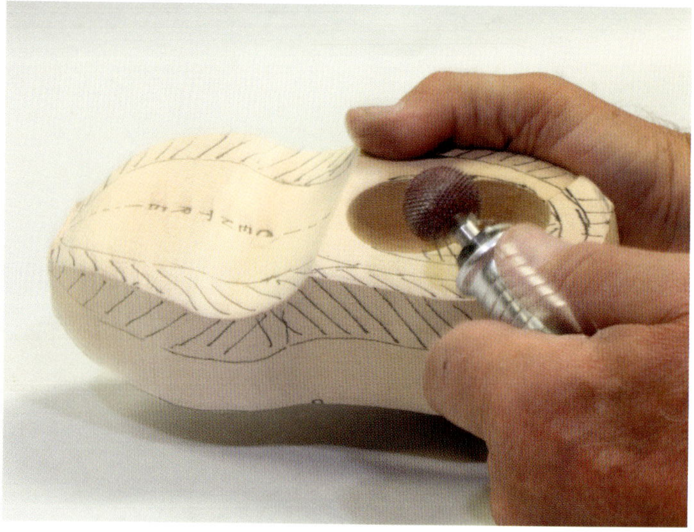

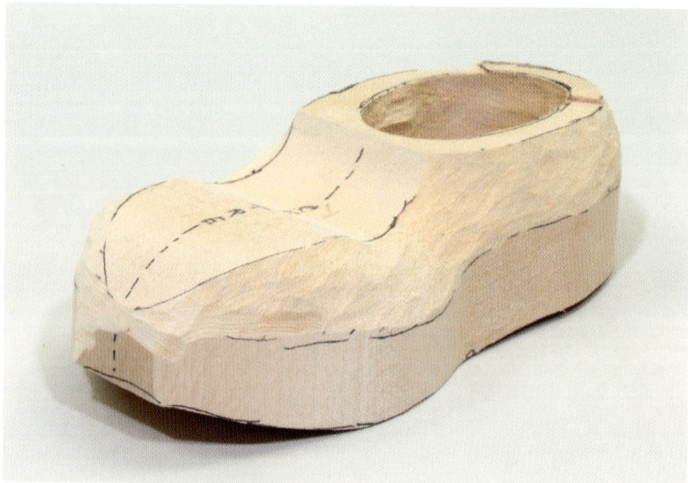

STEP 3: Rough carve the boot block. Draw in a center line along the length of the top line and, following the hash lines, start rounding the top of the boot using a ball-shaped carving burr. From the top of the boot, the vamp interior is cleared of any extra wood.

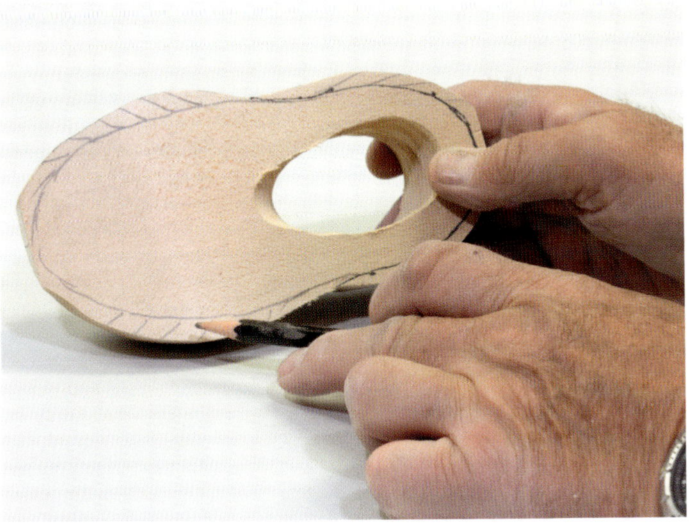

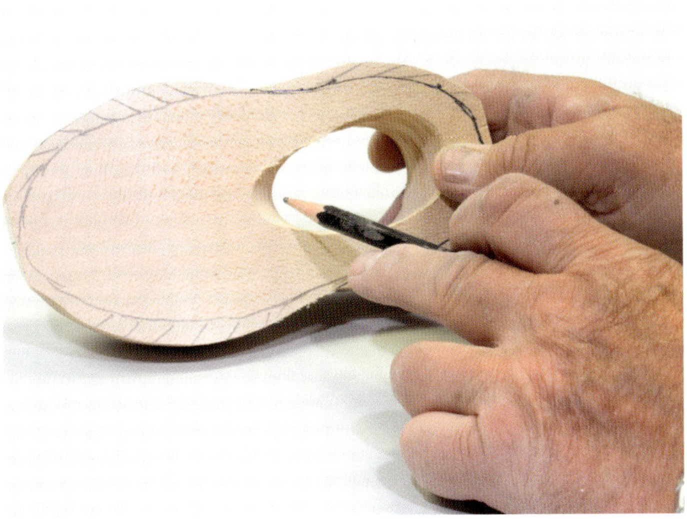

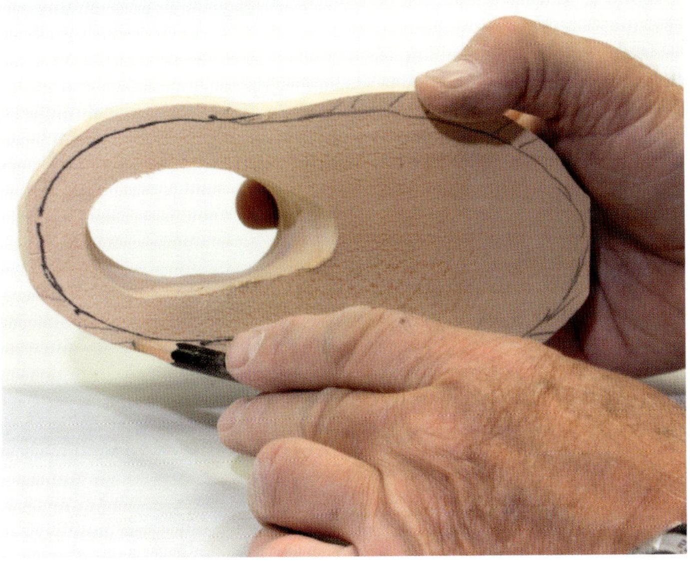

STEP 4: Draw in hash lines at bottom edge of the boot. Remove wood to show a slight rounding of the outer bottom edge. More inner vamp wood is removed from the bottom side, extending the hollowing process towards the toe area.

STEP 5: Carving the sole. With the shaping of the upper boot blank, it is now possible to get a clearer definition of the sole. Draw hash marks on the bottom side of the sole section and round the wood to show a 1/8" to 3/16" edge.

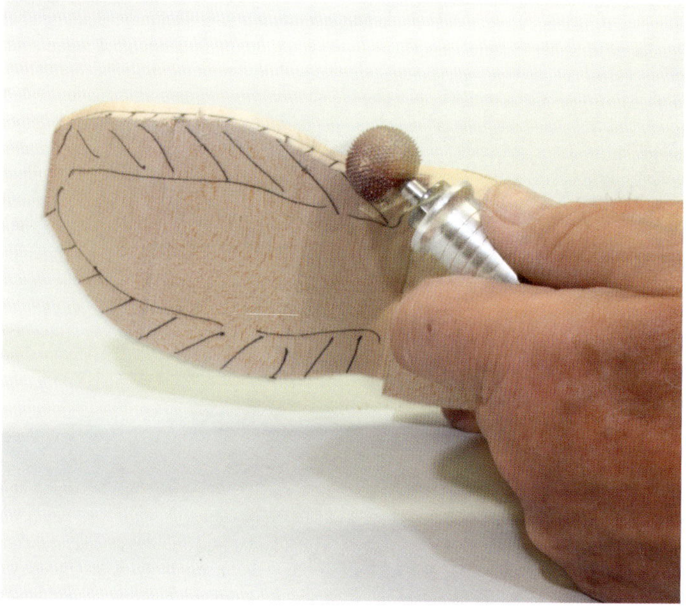

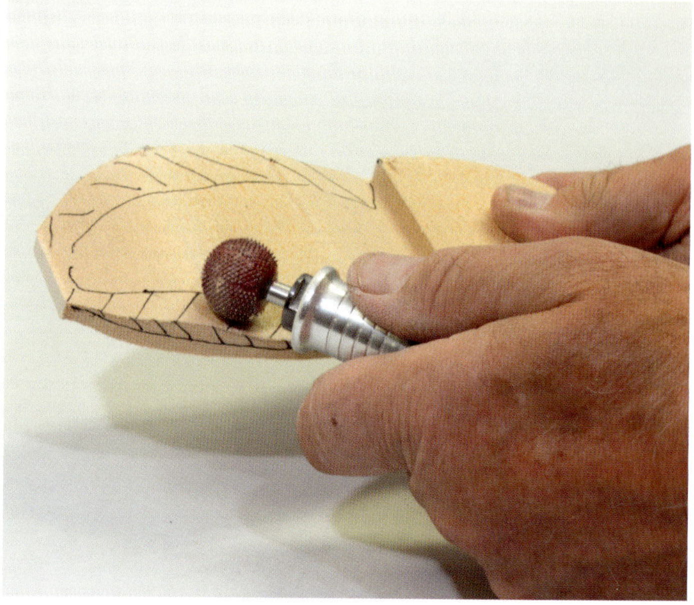

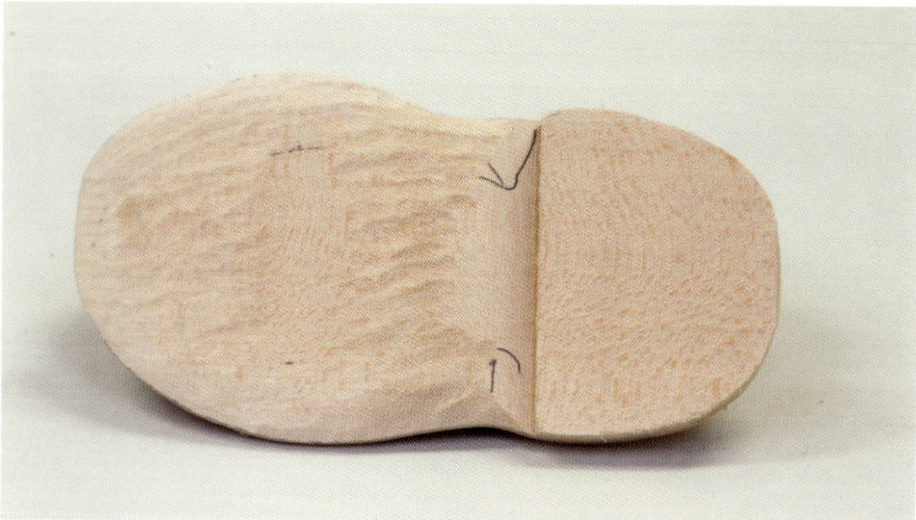

This edge is now ready for sanding.

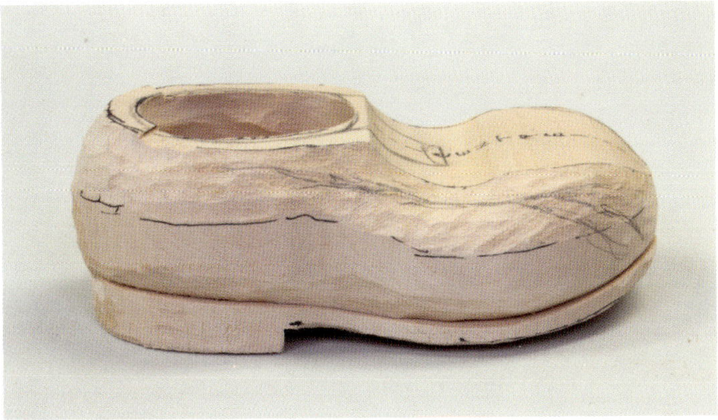

STEP 6: Refining and detailing. With a carving burr, the vamp is shaped to accommodate the toe and heel covers. Be sure to leave adequate wood to carve a reveal.

This reveal is the first definition of the toe and heal covers. Using a micro-motor carver with a ruby bit, the grooves form the first lines of demarcation.

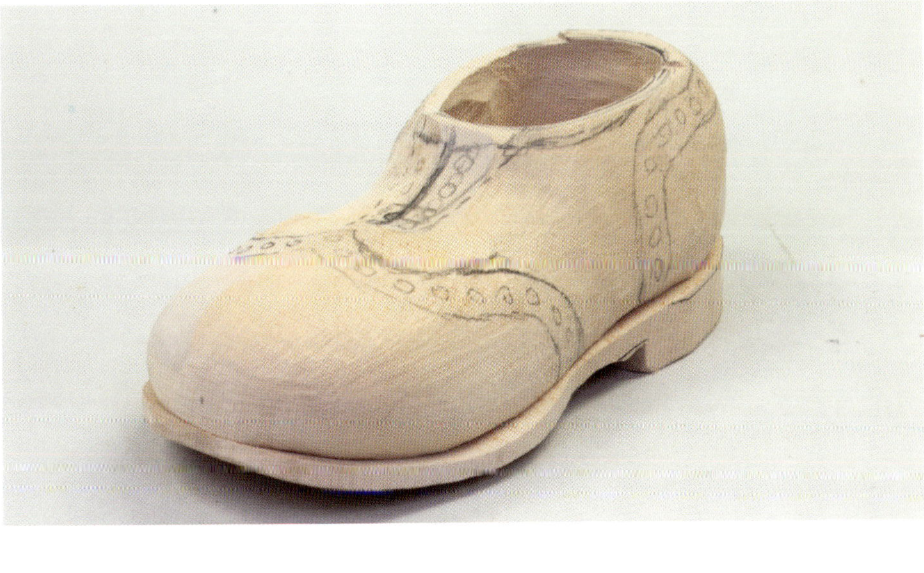

Sanding between each process allows one to redraw carving lines to define the details of the vamp.

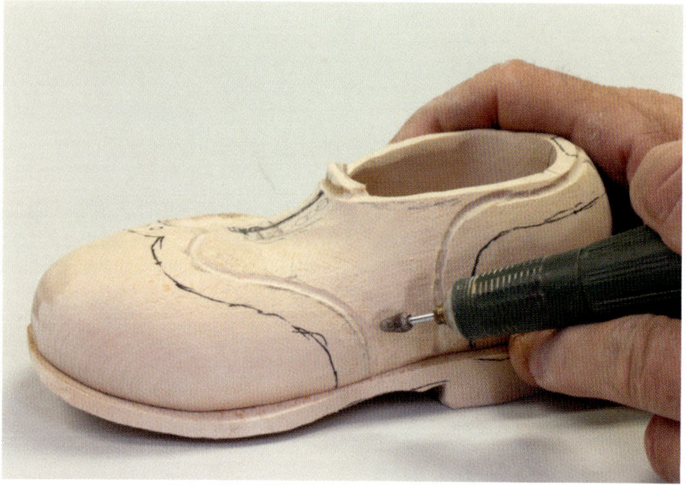

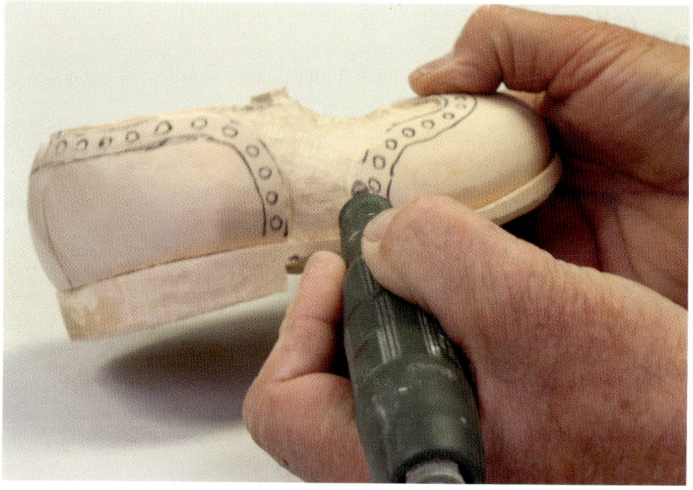

STEP 7: More reveal. Continuing with the ruby bit, more reveal is incorporated.

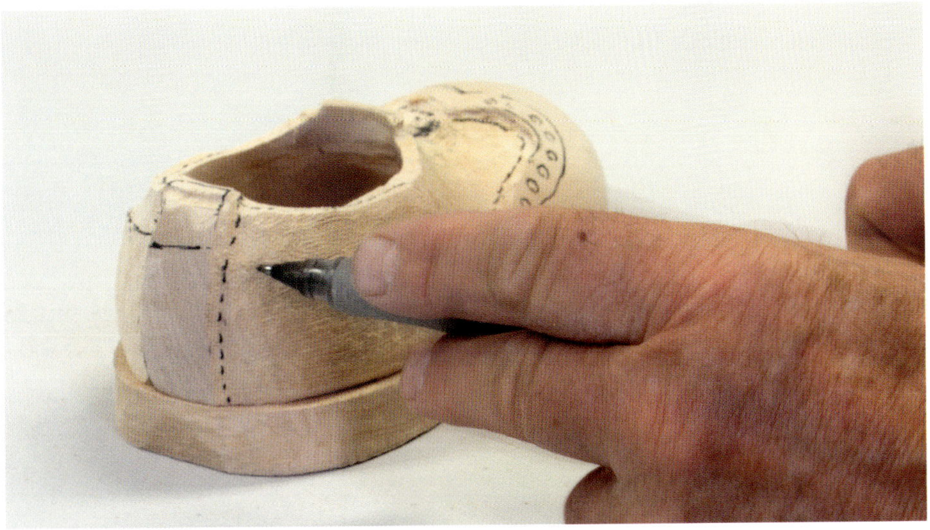

A heel strip is revealed and detailed.

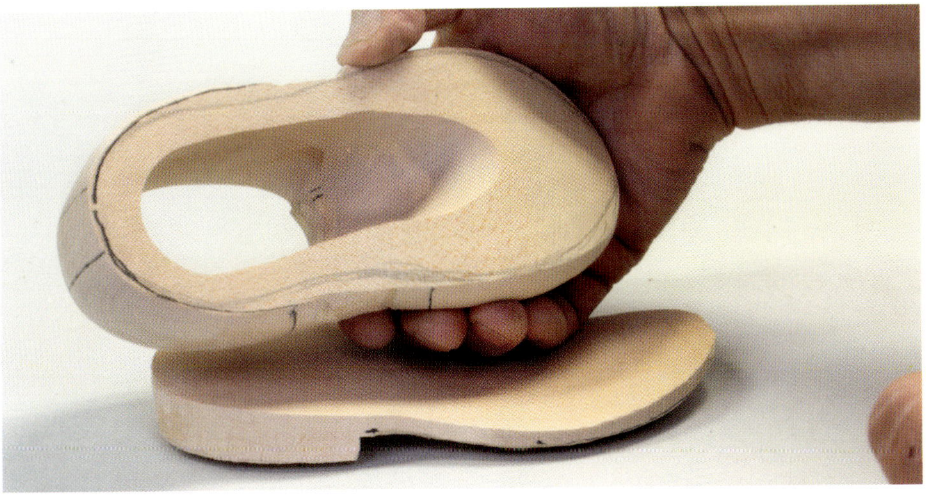

Throughout this step, the shoe vamp continues to be shaped and reduced in size.

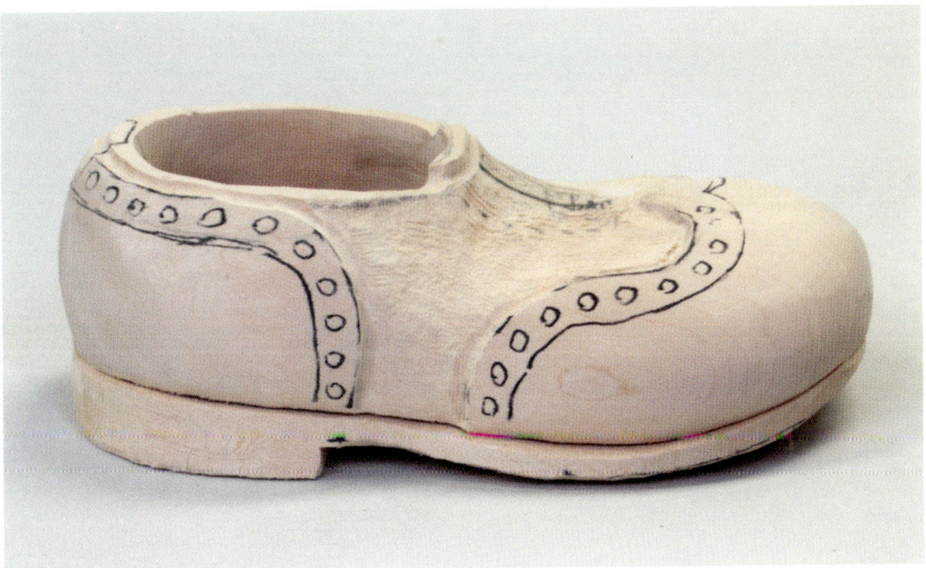

A quick sanding provides a smooth surface for the final details and texturing.

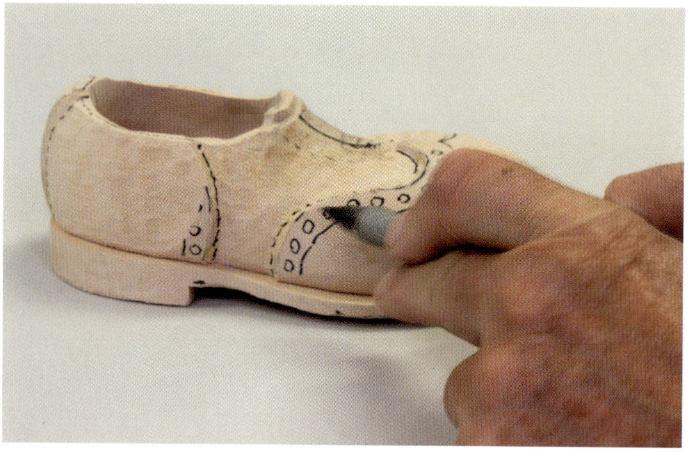

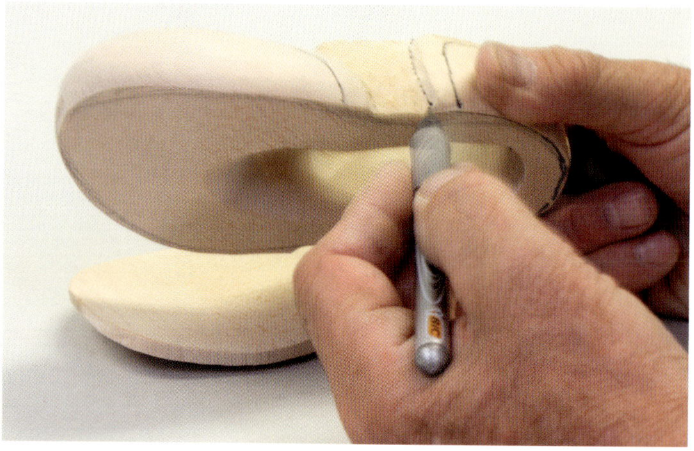

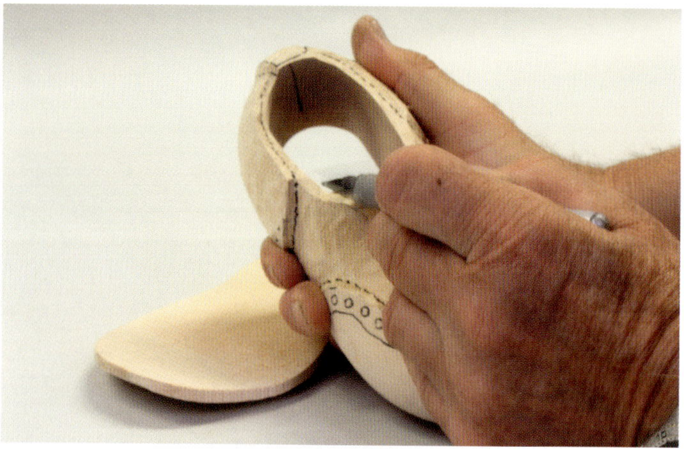

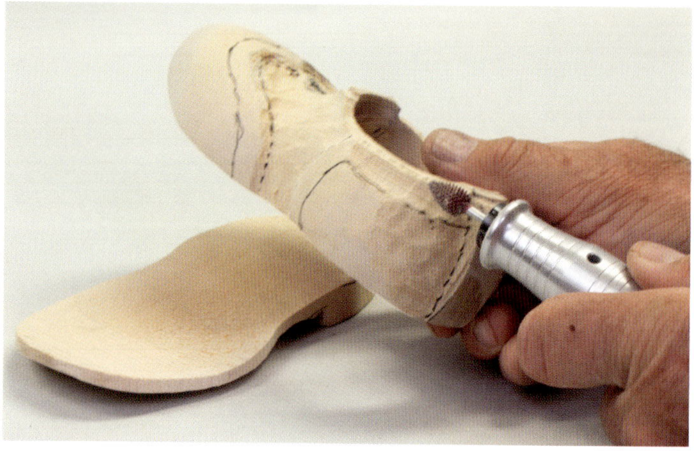

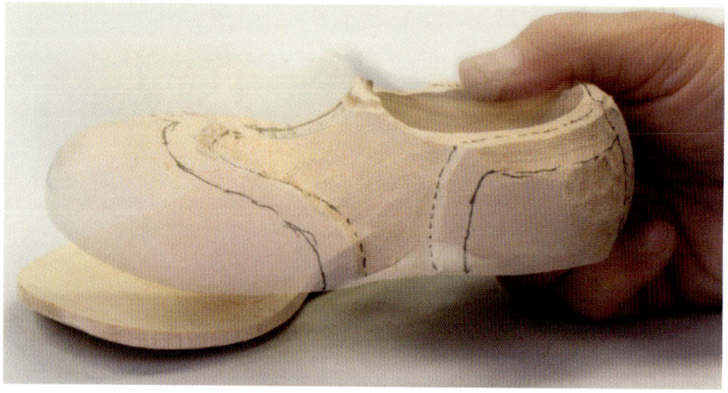

The texturing is done with a round ruby bit to show a contrast between the outer smooth surface and the inner textured surface.

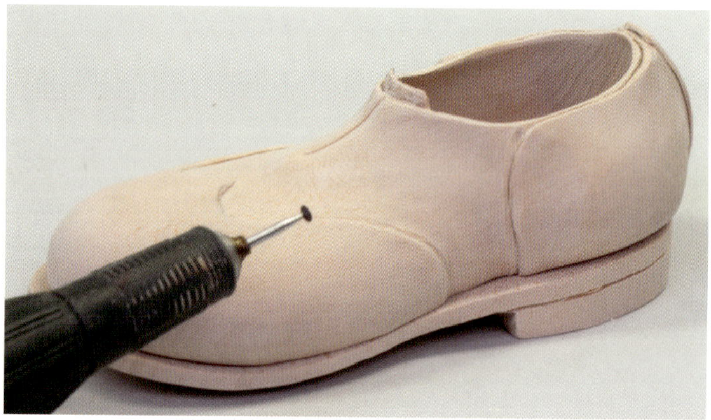

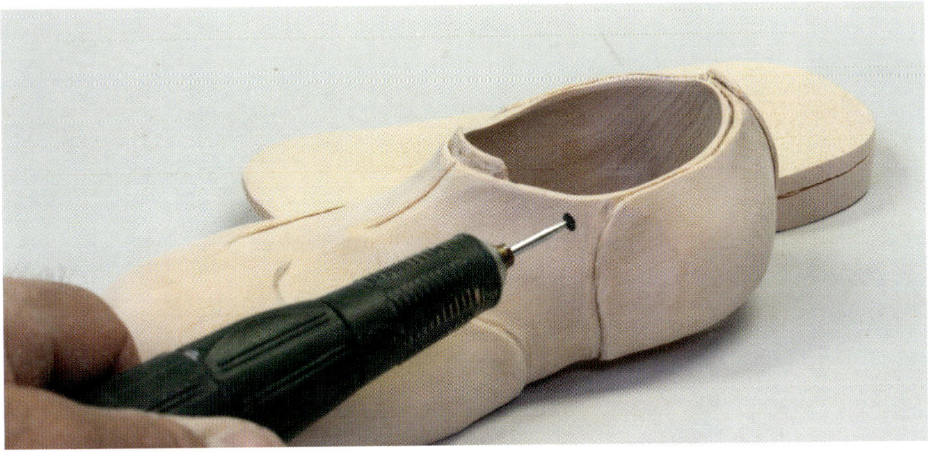

STEP 8: Reveal refinement. With a small diamond carving disc, the toe and heel cover reveals are cleaned up to show sharp, distinct edges.

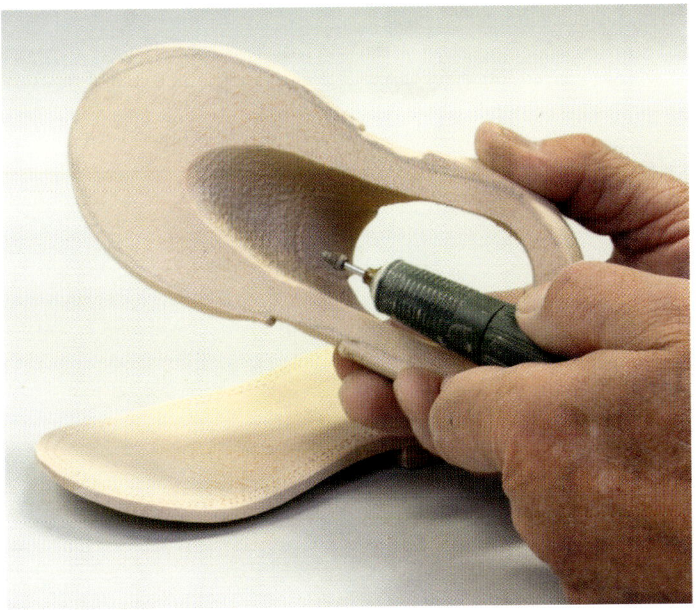

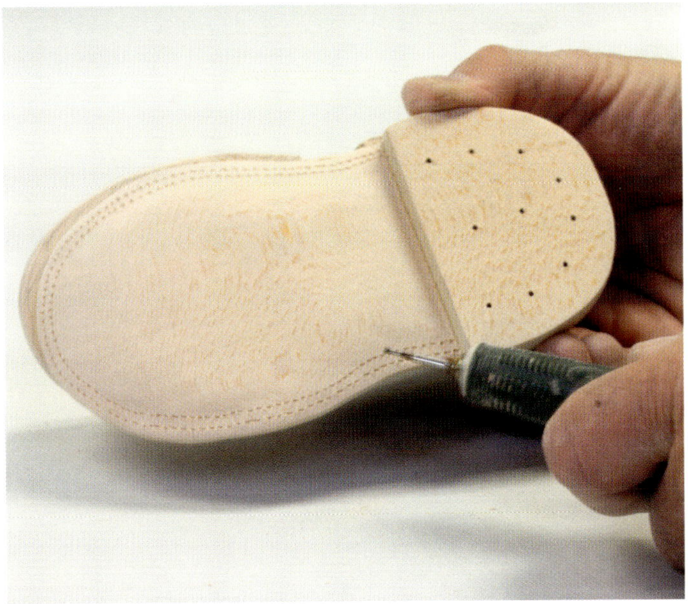

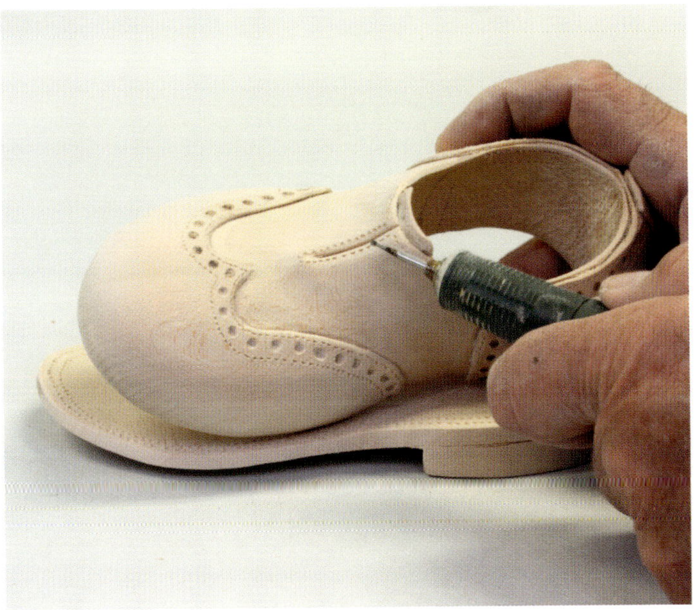

After a final sanding, thread details are carved with a small carbide bit.

STEP 9: Finishing. Apply sealant to the surface and sand to remove any rough edges.

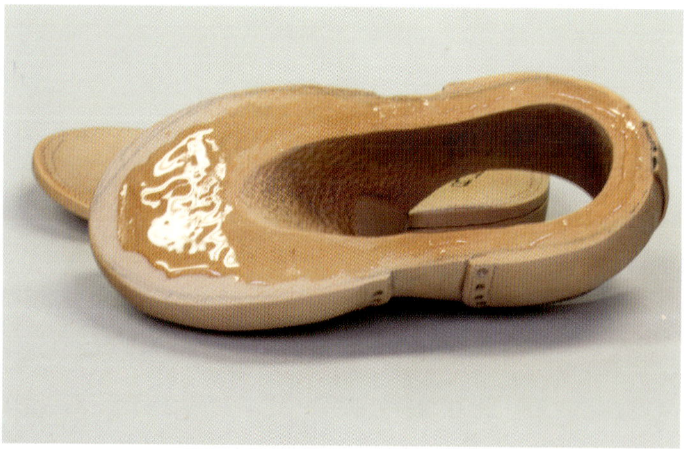

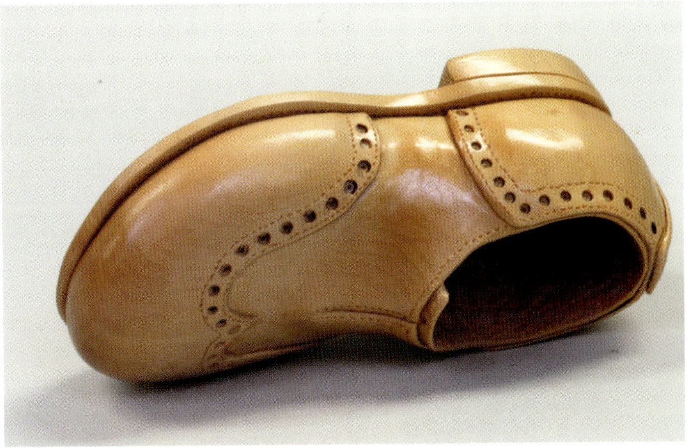

STEP 10: Re-assemble stage. Using a quick set, two-part epoxy glue, the boot can now be glued together.

Finish with a coat of clear varnish. Apply wax polish for a beautiful shine. Your project is complete.

Conclusion

Now, that the process to power-carving a "Roman style" wooden boot has been revealed, I hope that the trip you take on your boot- and shoe-making journey will be as exciting as it was for me in making the wren perch, Charlie, the brogues, and all the other shapes and sizes shown throughout this carving manual. Have a good trip.

Gallery

Spalted cedar

Diamond willow

Rocky Mountain juniper

Western flair, basswood, pine

Mayday, bark side

Mayday, smooth side

Pine boot

Patterns

BLOCK TO BLANK PROFILES

Points to Consider in Making a Pattern

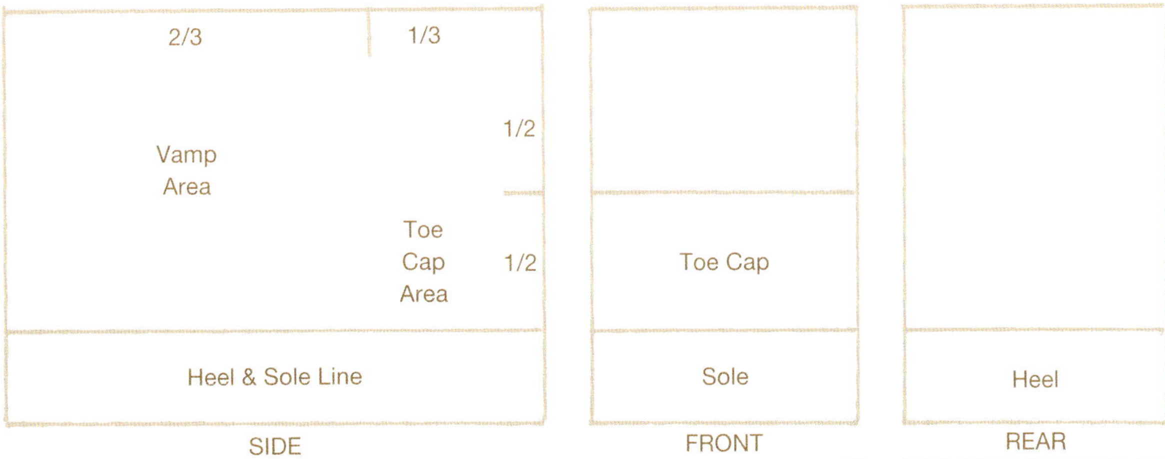

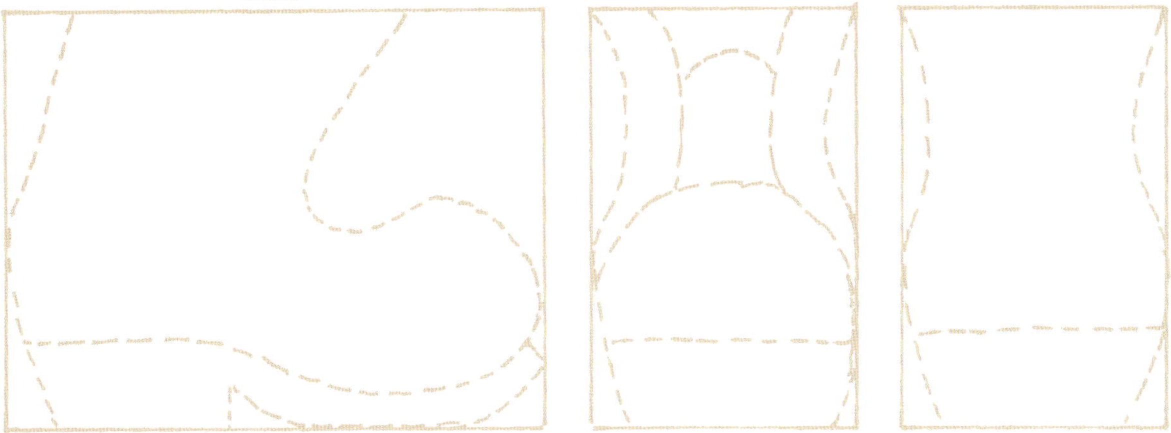

OUTLINES OF MODEL BOOT

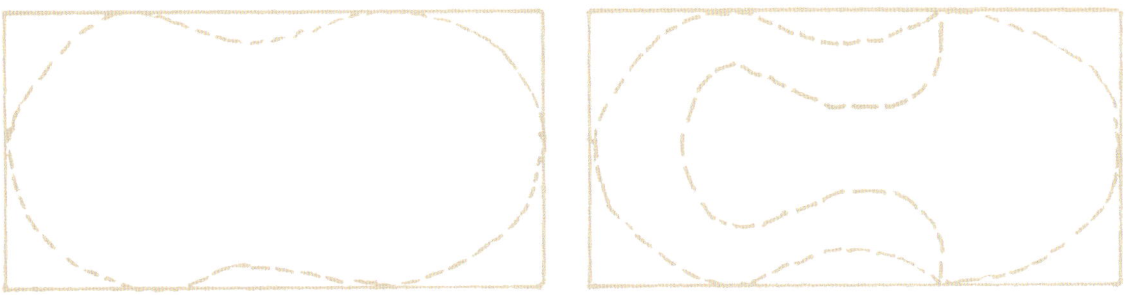

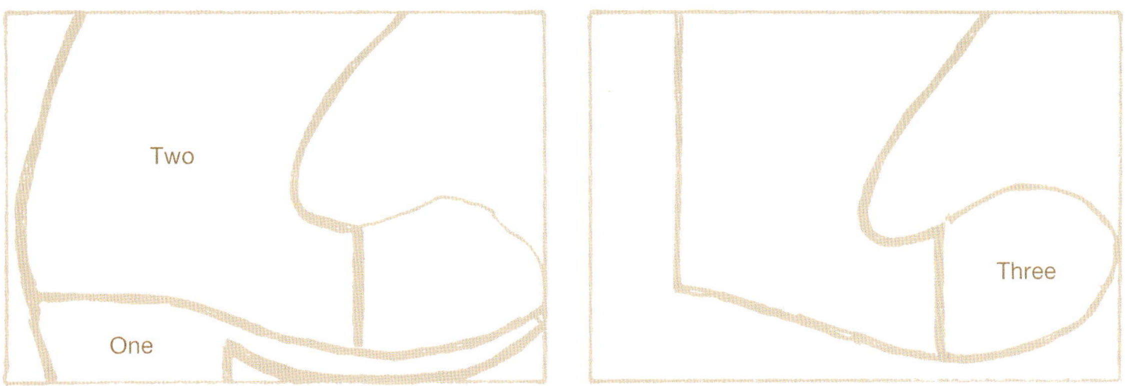

BLANK IN THREE PARTS

REFINING THE BLANK

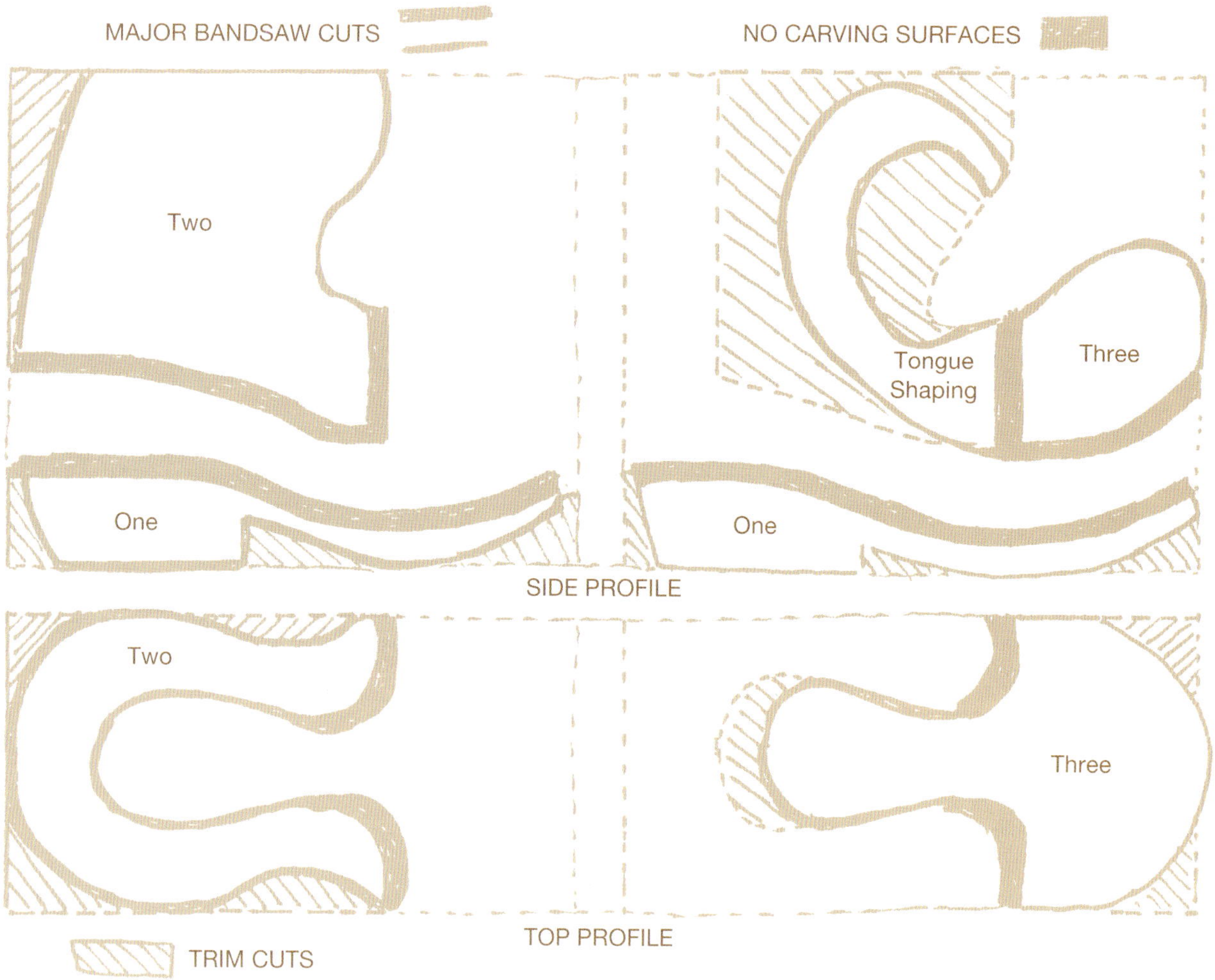

TOP VIEW BANDSAW CUT LINES

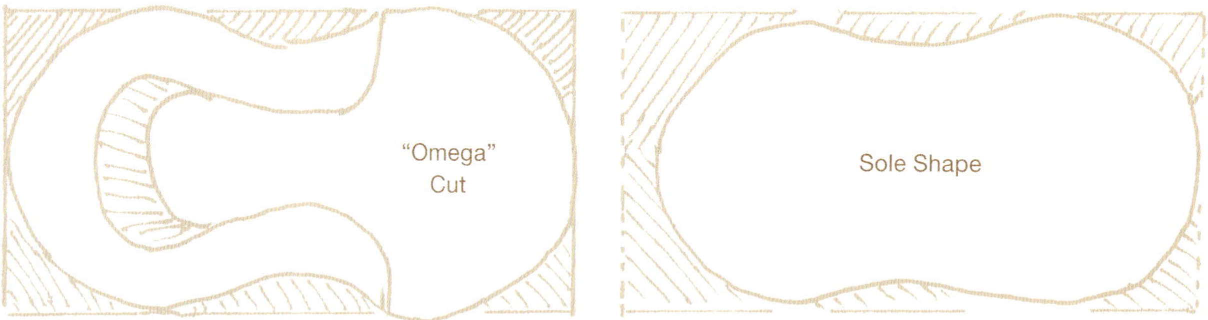

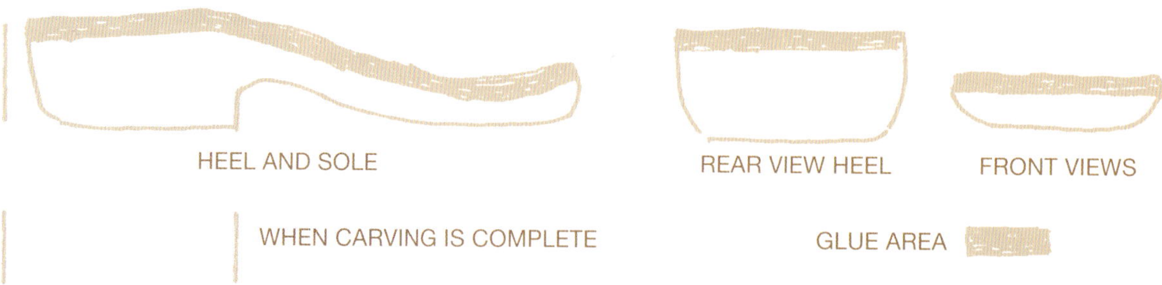

TONGUE SHAPING

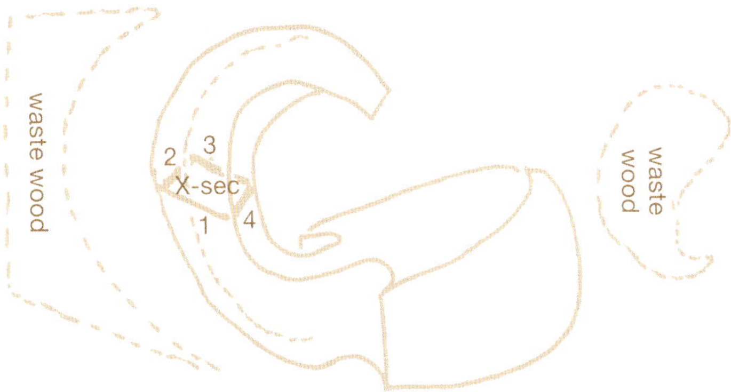

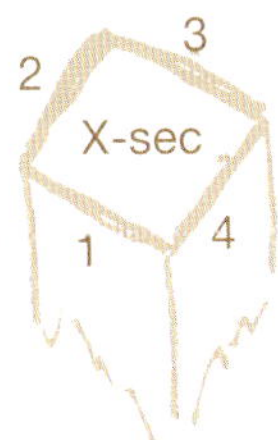

Cross section of tongue wood showing sides 1, 2, 3, 4

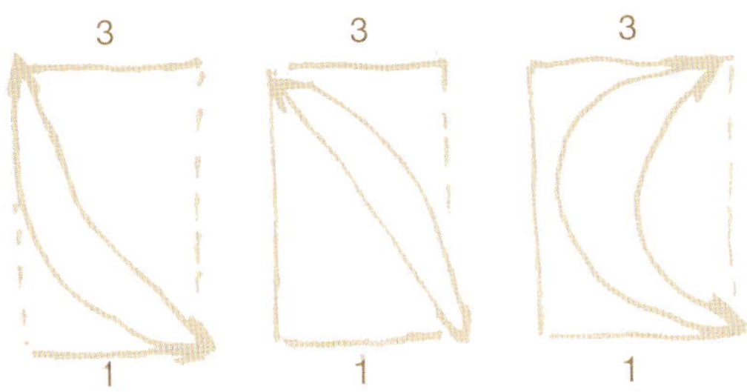

Options for tongue curvature by carving wood down to two edges

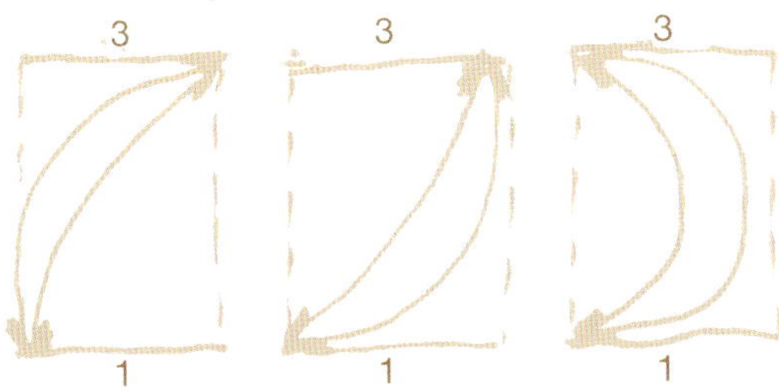

The amount of curvature and bend in the tongue depends on the amount of wood left in the initial cutting of the boot blank

WIDE OR NARROW

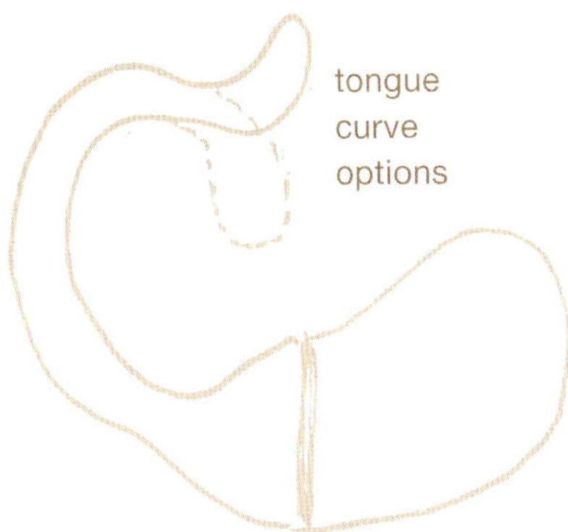

tongue curve options

UP OR DOWN CURVE

BANDSAW CUT LINES WHEN DESIGNING BOOT PATTERN

"MR. CASUAL1"

Separate Sole and THEN remove inner Vamp wood with a spade bit or Forstner bit.
Follow-up with Roughing and Shaping.

SHAPES AND VARIETIES

REVEALING, TEXTURING, DETAILING

WORK BOOT, REVEALED, TEXTURED, DECORATED

SHAPES & SIZES

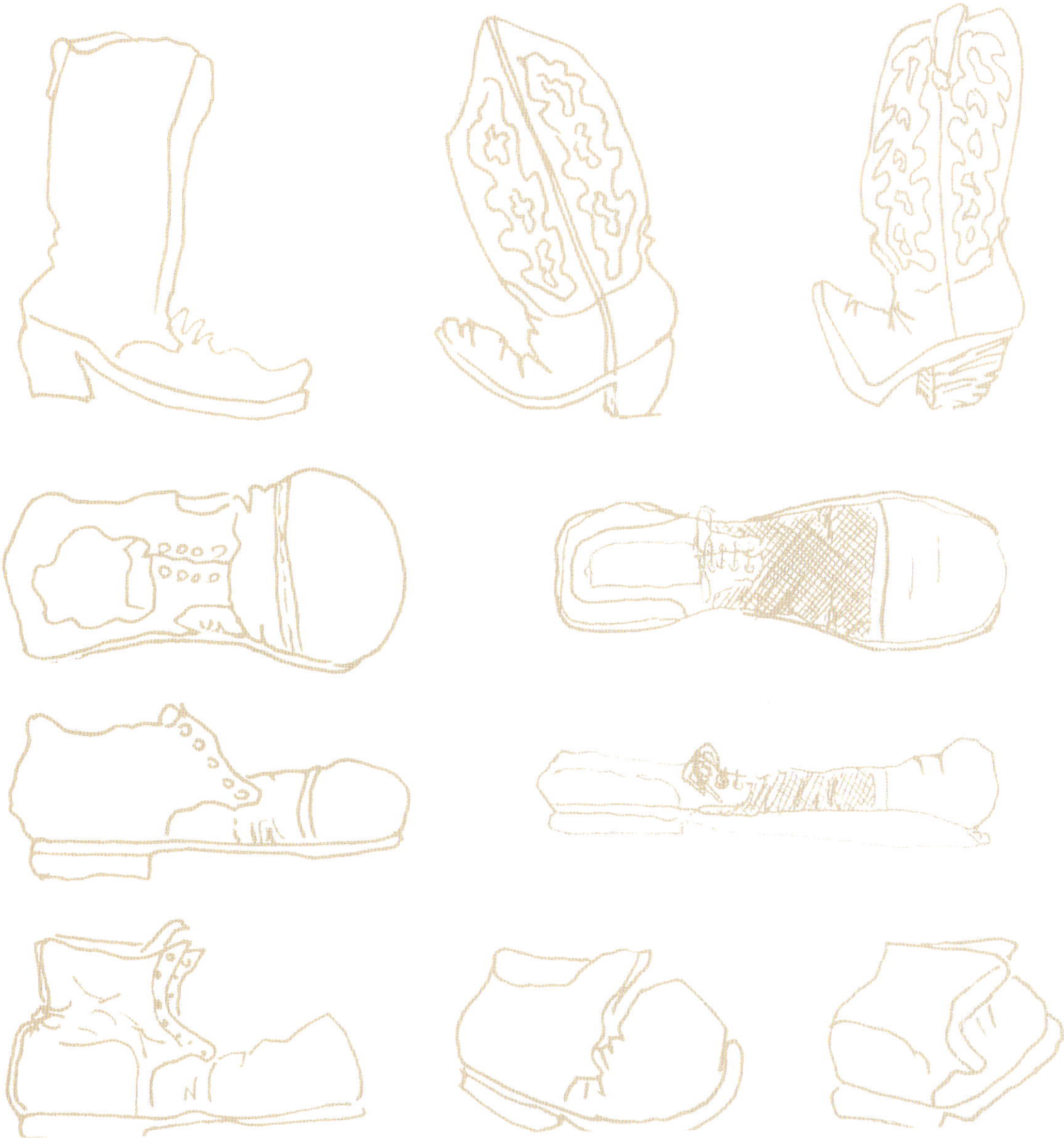

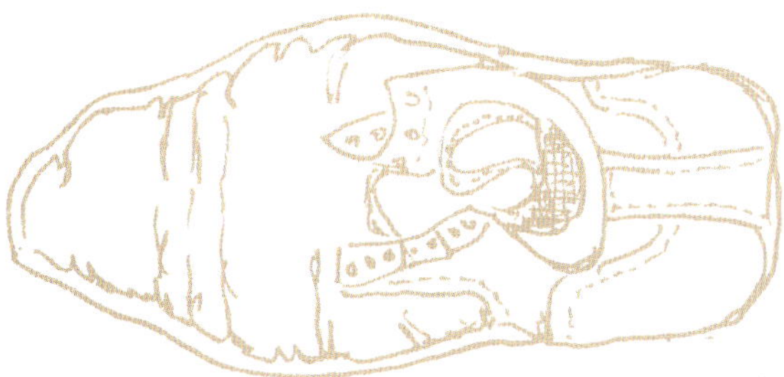

ROUGH
& TOUGH LIFE
—A MONUMENT!

DECORATING & THE FEMALE TOUCH!

WALKING ON WATER!